The Obama Syndrome

The Obama Syndrome

Surrender at Home, War Abroad

◆

TARIQ ALI

VERSO

London • New York

First published by Verso 2010
This updated paperback edition published by Verso 2011
© Tariq Ali 2011
Appendix 1 © Teri Reynolds 2010
All rights reserved

1 3 5 7 9 10 8 6 4 2

Verso
UK: 6 Meard Street, London W1F 0EG
US: 20 Jay Street, Suite 1010, Brooklyn, NY 11201
www.versobooks.com

Verso is the imprint of New Left Books

ISBN-13: 978-1-84467-757-3

British Library Cataloguing in Publication Data
A catalogue record for this book is available from the British Library

Library of Congress Cataloging-in-Publication Data
A catalog record for this book is available from the Library of Congress

Typeset in Bembo by MJ Gavan, Truro, Cornwall
Printed in the US by Quad/Graphics Fairfield

In Memoriam:

Howard Zinn
and
Daniel Bensaïd

CONTENTS

PREFACE

This essay is offered as a preliminary report on the first 1,000 days of the Obama presidency. Nothing more. It was written some months before the midterm elections that might well signal a further paralysis of the administration but also provide it with a formal excuse for moving further right and not undertaking any measures that might offend Republicans. It is already doing this, but things could get worse. These past two years of ineffective juggling have seen a continuation of the voodoo economics of the previous period, despite the collapse of the financial markets, the universal discrediting of the Wall Street system, and the worst economic crisis since the Great Depression, the effects of which have been delayed in the United States but are beginning to be felt in parts of Europe, old and new. The bungled and toothless "health care reform bill," drafted by insurance company lobbyists, was pushed through, but even this is likely to be ditched when costs explode soon after its implementation several years ahead. An important opportunity has been missed.

I intend to update this volume in time for the renomination and the 2012 campaign, but perhaps it won't be necessary as other books, sharper and more distinctive in tone, take its place, necessary antidotes to the gushing biographies that compete in their worship of power. Best in these times not to be intimidated by victors or brutish auxiliaries who place their heel on the intellect while their tongues easily move into places once occupied by their rivals.

My thanks for all their help to colleagues Kenta Tsuda and Tom Mertes at *New Left Review*; Jacob Stevens, Mark Martin, Rowan Wilson and Sebastian Budgen at Verso Books; and Anthony Arnove and Brenda Coughlin in New York.

In conclusion, a few words for aficionados on the typeface used for this book. Given that some might regard this essay as far too inflammatory already, I decided to abandon my tried and trusted Fournier since it might overheat the text. Instead I chose the slightly cooler and more refined Bembo, a gift from the Italian Renaissance. Pietro Bembo's (1470–1547) own *Gli Asolini* was dedicated to Lucretia Borgia, whose name a French scholar claimed was an "occupant le verso du titre." Pietro, too, liked verso. More to the point it was Bembo who gave the publisher Aldus the idea for the small format of his books, also appropriate, I thought, for this book. Furthermore Bembo also devised the anchor-and-dolphin, the best known of printer's marks. As a pioneering editor, Pietro Bembo established strict standards, insisted on proper punctuation and was scathing of sloppy publishing. New Left Books, the progenitors of Verso, regarded him as a patron saint when they set up shop forty years ago.

Tariq Ali
June 2010

It isn't a president who can help or hurt; it's the system. And this system is not only ruling us in America, it is ruling the world. Nowadays, when a man is running for president of the United States, he is not running for president of the United States alone; he has to be acceptable to other areas of the world where American influence rules ... The only thing that made him [Lyndon Baines Johnson] *acceptable to the world was that the shrewd capitalists, the shrewd imperialists, knew that the only way people would run towards the fox would be if you showed them a wolf. So they created a ghastly alternative.*

Malcolm X, Paris, November 23, 1964

1

AN UNPRECEDENTED
HISTORICAL EVENT

Three decades ago when Ronald Reagan was elected president of the United States, it was difficult for most progressive observers to imagine that the actor-celebrity's period in office would mark the beginnings of a new consensus at home and abroad, and the slow dismantling of the New Deal as well as the Soviet Union. They could not believe that a dimwitted, second-rate actor could accomplish anything. A minority suggested otherwise. In a remarkably prescient essay, Mike Davis, writing in his inimitable style a few months after Reagan's inauguration, predicted that California-style politics was the future writ large:

> Like the beast of the apocalypse, Reaganism has slouched out of the Sunbelt, devouring liberal senators and Great Society programs in its path. With the fortieth president's popularity rating soaring above 80 percent (partially thanks to an inept assassin), most surviving liberals seem frightened out of their moral fibers. Pragmatic as well as right-leaning Democrats have joined with Republicans in a new "era of good feeling," slashing vital welfare spending to make way for the biggest and most ominous escalation of arms spending in history. Public discourse has been commandeered by multitudes of "post-liberals," "neo-conservatives" and "new rightists" who offer

the grotesque ideological inversion of positive discrimination for the middle classes and welfare for the corporations. Indisputably a seismic shift rightwards is taking place at every level of American politics with grim implications for the future.[1]

The New Democrats embraced Reaganism on virtually every level. Clinton had neither the political desire nor the will to push back any of the Reagan "reforms." W. Bush built on the foundations laid by Reagan, increasing the social and economic disparities between the rich and the less well-off sections of the population. The poor were ignored by most politicians, permitted a few meager handouts, encouraged to eat junk food and grow obese and then were denied health care. A neoliberal Malthusianism had become the order of the day. And Obama?

Once the novelty of the candidate and the high-octane campaign had worn off, a dull Republican rival and his more spirited Alaskan snowbilly had been safely dispatched, and the mixed-race president was safely and happily ensconced in the White House, the starlit night disappeared and a confused, misty gray half light enveloped the country once again. Stern reality interrupted the celebrations. The situation at home and abroad was bleak. The first hundred days revealed that no regeneration was in sight. As the wars in Iraq and Afghanistan showed few signs of subsiding, the Orwellian mediasphere continued to proclaim "peace is war" and "war is peace."

More worryingly for most Americans, the economic storm at home was threatening to develop into a hurricane. Here was a rare chance for a strong political leader with a set of more progressive

1   Mike Davis, "The Rise of the New Right," *New Left Review*, July/August 1981, 128.

2

values than his predecessors to move forward swiftly and establish a new agenda. In *Dreams from My Father*, the author had referred to Malcolm X's character in glowing terms: "the blunt poetry of his words, his unadorned insistence on respect, promised a new and uncompromising order, martial in its discipline, forged through sheer force of will." Alas, no such leader existed now.

On the economic front, the Bush bailouts had temporarily saved the Wall Street banker, but at a huge cost. The effect on the country at large was to create fear, as low-income families saw new vistas of poverty and misery threatening their lives. Some found solace in the collective nuttiness of Tea Party libertarianism. California, once the headquarters of the neoliberal new-technology miracle, was bankrupt. Arizona's Republican leaders were planning to give the police new powers to deal with "immigrants," engendering an atmosphere that could easily lead to an anti-Hispanic *Kaktusnacht*. The corporations, especially those linked to oil, were busy getting their way by exercising what the late Ida Tarbell (an early scourge of the petroleum industry with no mainstream equivalent in these great times) used to describe as a combination of force, deceit, fraud, bribery, gross illegality, intimidation and terror. She wrote those words in the bad old days of Standard Oil. Today we could add to her list one-sided negotiations, unrestricted lobbying and light-touch regulation. Reagan-time had prepared a secure hive to attract swarms of corporate criminals who soon became central figures in the new economy and laid the foundations of a new Enron that led to the 2008 collapse.

The Reagan counter-reforms—embraced first by Clinton and now by Obama—further institutionalized business control over social interest. In 1985, the historian Stephanie Coontz wrote a sharp critique of the Democrats for failing to challenge and provide an alternative to the predatory capitalism unleashed by the Reagan administration; she pointed out how deep the rot had gone by highlighting the role of the American Bar Association in preparing public laws and making available the staff to administer them:

> It's instructive to make a list of recent chairmen of the law-drafting committees of the ABA and of the clients they have represented: the Chairman of the Committee on Environmental Controls was a lawyer for Humble Oil and General Motors; the Drug Law Committee was headed by an employee of the Pharmaceutical Manufacturer's Association; the Aviation Law Committee by an Eastern Airlines executive; the Committee on Railroads by the vice-president and general counsel of Gulf Mobile and Ohio Railroad Company; the Section on Anti-Trust Laws by an IBM and Shell Oil executive; the Section on Public Utility Law by an AT&T employee; the Beverage Law Committee by a lawyer for Coca-Cola.[2]

This reality, difficult to parody, continues to throttle popular sovereignty, but is now considered normal, an unchallengeable pillar of Democracy Inc. And to anyone out there who still thinks that the trendy, cool new IT companies are any better when it comes to buying influence to protect their interests, I recommend a reading of Robert Reich:

> Until Google went public in August 2004, it took pride in being a maverick outsider. But once it became a multi-billion-dollar public company, it needed to become part of

---

2 Stephanie Coontz, "No Alternative: Reagan's Reelection and the Democratic Party," *The Year Left: An American Socialist Yearbook*, edited by Mike Davis, Fred Pfiel and Michael Sprinker, New York, 1985.

the Washington establishment. In 2005, it spent more than $500,000 hiring lobbying firms and consultants. Google had no choice. Yahoo, Microsoft, Apple, and a gaggle of telecom companies were already well represented in Washington. In 2005 alone, Microsoft spent almost $9 million on lobbying, and its executives donated millions more to politicians on both sides of the aisle. The competitive positions of every one of these companies, relative to one another, would be influenced by decisions made in Washington on issues ranging from intellectual capital, antitrust, international trade, and relations with China.[3]

The dismantling of controls, which had never been challenged during the Clinton years, proceeded apace. Each financial scandal was treated as an exception, its authors bad apples that had been removed. The real problem was that the entire barrel was rotten. But Obama, far from posing any threat to the neoliberals, boasted of his links to the rich, "savvy" Wall Street CEOs.[4] US capitalism had turned everything into a commodity, including the country's politicians, with this difference: the human commodities knew who owned them, and they behaved accordingly.

Had all the visions of change, progress and new direction been an optical illusion? "No" was the first reaction of the liberal

3 Robert Reich, "Everyday Corruption," *The American Prospect*, June 21, 2010.
4 David Bromwich, one of Obama's supporters at Yale, rebuked him in a "Diary" note in the May 13, 2010 edition of *London Review of Books*: "He was new to the national elite and enjoyed his membership palpably. This came out in debates and town meetings where he often mentioned that the profits from his books had lodged him in the highest tax bracket. It would emerge later in his comment on Lloyd Blankfein and Jamie Dimon, the CEOs of Goldman Sachs and JPMorgan: 'I know both those guys; they are very savvy businessmen.' One can't imagine Franklin Roosevelt or John Kennedy saying such a thing, or wanting to say it. They had known 'those guys' all their lives and felt no tingle of reflected glory. Obama has not yet recognised that his conspicuous relish of his place among the elite does him two kinds of harm: it spurs resentment in people lower down the ladder; and it diminishes his stature among the grandees by showing that he needs them."

pundits, impressed by the high-pressure salesmanship now on offer and using the Tea Party/Fox symbiosis as permanent blackmail. If there was anyone who could sell the system and its rational needs to a skeptical world it was the new president. Democrats, the alpha and omega of whose political philosophy was to manage the system better, now controlled the country. They would introduce badly needed reforms in order to modernize it and assure its harmonious development. The lessons of Clinton's failures, epitomized by Lawrence Summers's appointment to the Treasury, had been fully learned and absorbed. Where there had been discord there would now be amity. The problem, they pleaded, was not Obama but the Democrats who dominated Congress and Senate. All that was needed was time. But the economic emergency required emergency measures and the war in Afghanistan was going from bad to worse. The time was now. That is what the crowds had chanted at Obama's rallies in the first and more political of his two campaigns, when his opponents were Bill and Hillary Clinton. The honeymoon did not last too long.

With politics going to the dogs in most parts of the world (South America was a striking exception) and serious political columnists resorting to the clichés of airport thrillers, the first campaign had succeeded in galvanizing a generation of young Americans across the class and race divide. They believed their candidate was capable of correcting the imbalances and of reversing the turbo-charged thrust of corporate power and its adjuncts at home, while throwing the imperial juggernaut abroad into reverse. Who could blame them? Their enthusiasm was infectious. Traveling through the United States in 2007–8 was an unusual experience. Any expression of skepticism on my part (or that of other graybeards) was greeted with disbelief and sometimes anger.

How could their candidate be charming, calm, intelligent, but also perfidious? Their enthusiasm refused any coupling with criticism. They did not wish to see Obama as a creature mired in the political culture of a corrupted and cynical Democratic Party—and that, too, in Chicago—or a politician who had no desire to prize himself loose from the corporate political system that had assisted his rise to the presidency. Many believed that if Obama were elected, the country and its citizens would move on and part company with the murderous wars and the domestic politics of the Bush–Cheney period. Sadly, a different destiny lay ahead.

Forty acres and a mule at home and peace abroad were, of course, never on the agenda, and to be fair, Obama did not pledge anything remotely resembling such a project—or even a new New Deal. Bill Clinton was way off the mark in suggesting that the Obama campaign was merely a repeat of Jesse Jackson's bid in 1984. The Rainbow Coalition that had united progressives inside and outside the structures of the Democratic Party that year was quite remarkable at the time and looks even more so in retrospect. Its aim was to challenge and breach the Reagan consensus. Jackson's program promised a 25 percent reduction in the defense budget and a bilateral nuclear weapons freeze; the billions of dollars saved by the reductions in arms spending to be reallocated to human needs, through creating a social infrastructure that would benefit the poor; and normalized relations with Cuba and an end to US military interventions in Central America, the Caribbean and the Middle East. Not surprisingly, he did not win the nomination, but with virtually no TV advertising and a tiny amount of money compared with the others, he still won the primaries in DC, Louisiana, South Carolina, Mississippi and Virginia, obtaining almost 20 percent of the total Democratic primary votes and 80 percent of all African American votes. This was the swan song of the civil rights generation. Bill Clinton had hoped that Obama's early wins might peter out in the same way, but here he underestimated his wife's opponent. He failed to understand that very little separated the politics espoused by the man from Chicago from those defended by the Clintons. In the old days the race card would have done the trick, but not this time. The candidate from the South Side was very much a post–civil rights politician.

Obama did not dampen the hopes of youthful partisans who chose to interpret the marketing slogans "Change we can believe in" or the even more vacuous "Yes, we can" as a promise of something real. The aim of this type of sloganeering is to win support without offering anything in return except fine words, and on that level the new chief is a master. Truth in such campaigning is usually a bystander. Little of what Obama actually said in a combination of blandishments, special pleading and specious arguments justified much optimism, but the manner of his speaking, the color of his skin and the constant invocation of the word "change" helped create a new spirit in the country—Obamania—that propelled him to the White House. He won seven million more votes than his opponent, even though this share of the popular vote did not register a huge increase over those of his recent predecessors, as had appeared possible at one stage. A layer of white Democrats stayed at home, but their absence was balanced by the turnout of independent voters, the majority of whom voted for the Democrat. Whether they will still do so in the 2010 midterms remains an open question.

The Obama Effect was enhanced by the fact that both Obama's person and his ultramoderate views were anathema to the repellent anchors on Fox TV and the crazed bigots of radio talk shows. If *they* hated him, he *must* be fine. What better way to combat the age of fanaticism and propaganda than to elect a young, bright, handsome African American and his equally attractive and intelligent African American spouse and send them in to occupy the White House and cleanse it of dust and cobwebs? It was difficult to remain unmoved by a political enthusiasm that—unlike the hoopla of Wall Street—was without ulterior motives. It was occasioned by a growing disgust with the corruptions of Empire, the officially sanctioned torture, the imprisonment without trial in foreign lands, and the waterboarding so admired by Bush apologists in the media, the most publicity-seeking of whom tried out a designer version and found it not too bad. Trying a spell in Bagram prison (the site of a deregulated, free-for-all torture system outside Kabul) disguised as a bearded Afghan was the obvious next step, but here his imagination failed him.

Add to all this the ease with which politicians auctioned themselves to the lobby system, with selected lobbyists themselves helping to draft new laws that favored their interests, and the canvas is virtually complete. The young who campaigned for Obama did so because they regarded Bush and Cheney as amoral and venal politicians who represented the "haves and have-mores" at home and murder abroad. They did not like the fork-tongued language of the Clintons with its slanted references and its soft-touch racism. In Obama, they thought, at long last they had found a leader who was not going to put the face of reason on wickedness or achieve supposedly reputable ends by disreputable means. He would be a righteous ruler. The candidate encouraged this view.

I happened to be in New York when Obama made the cleverest speech in the battle for the White House, an explanation of the outspoken anti-imperialist sermons of his former pastor, Reverend Jeremiah Wright, in the Trinity United Church of Christ, which the Obamas had attended for many years. It was the only time in the campaign American citizens were not treated as stupefied kids. The effect was electric. The speech became an immediate topic for street discussions.

Naturally, Obama confessed, he had always disagreed with those views. Naturally. Nonetheless he sought to contextualize them: they were the result of *old* and deep-seated bitternesses that grew out of the African American condition:

> I can no more disown him than I can disown the black community. I can no more disown him than my white grandmother—a woman who helped raise me, a woman who sacrificed again and again for me, a woman who loves me as much as she loves anything in this world, but a woman who once confessed her fear of black men who passed by her on the street, and who on more than one occasion has uttered racial or ethnic stereotypes that made me cringe. These people are a part of me. And they are a part of America, this country that I love.

It was clever. It worked. Underlying it was a sleight of hand: Wright was supposedly angered by *past* injustices, and everyone could agree on that.

After all, most in the United States, except for the deranged, now agree (at least in public) that lynching black people was not a good thing. If the anger was related to past sins alone, then few could blame the pastor. He belonged to a generation that had suffered. But Wright's depiction of present-day America as a land of triple evil—economic inequality, structural racism and imperial militarism—was "unacceptable," "divisive," "distorted," "inexcusable" and failed to note the changes that had taken place of which the most striking was Barack Obama's own campaign to become president. What was also "profoundly distorted," according to Obama, was Wright's view "that sees the conflicts in the Middle East as rooted primarily in the actions of stalwart allies like Israel, instead of emanating from the perverse and hateful ideologies of radical Islam." The public was not enlightened on whence radical Islam had emanated.

Nor was there much discussion of the condition of African Americans today, in the twenty-first century. Much has changed, including the ethnic makeup of the American prison population: for the first fifty years of the last century, whites constituted 70 percent of prisoners. In 2000 they were well under 30 percent. Their place had mostly been taken by young African Americans. The arrest rates for whites and blacks remained stable; it was the incarceration ratio that had altered dramatically. Statistics demonstrated that a majority of African Americans from poor families faced the prospect of time in prison.[5] Nor was this a secret, and it was one reason among many that explained the hatred most African American communities felt for Ronald Reagan.

In a deliberately provocative response, Wright challenged Obama and the implication that there was little to upset African Americans in the twenty-first century, making it clear that his views had not altered.[6] Obama now broke off all relations with the

5 In an arresting survey, Loïc Wacquant, a prominent sociologist, wrote: "A short thirty-five years after the Civil Rights movement finally gained African Americans effective access to the voting booth, a full century after Abolition, this right is being taken back by the penal system via legal dispositions that are of dubious constitutional validity and violate in many cases (notably lifetime disenfranchisement) international conventions on human rights ratified by the United States." "The First Prison Society," *New Left Review*, January/February 2002.
6 This was the signal for making him a nonperson, as used to happen in the Soviet Union during the 1930s. It was Northwestern University that led the way with a

turbulent priest and binned that section of his past. He preferred the praise of good thinking people. Orlando Patterson duly obliged, hailing the new presidency as the beginning of a "cultural Reformation" that would lead to integration on every level. Numerous others followed suit: black celeb magazines with their women-as-sex-object covers praised him for discouraging promiscuity; some wrote of how the president and Michelle were forcing black men to consider marriage at an early stage. Why just black men? Are they genetically incapable of sustained relationships, unlike their white counterparts? The statistics do not justify this form of self-flagellation. In this arena class plays a more significant role than race. Meanwhile reports began to pour in from Stakhanovite school officials in New Orleans claiming that since the victory and with Obama's pleasing face beaming from every classroom wall the achievement gap between black and white students was rapidly narrowing. This turned out not to be the case, but it was a nice idea. At least school officials in the newly privatized schools were emulating Mao-style voluntarism.

---

weasel statement on May 1, 2008: "Earlier this academic year, acting on the recommendation of faculty committees, Northwestern University extended an invitation to the Rev. Dr. Jeremiah Wright, former senior minister of Trinity United Church of Christ in Chicago, to receive an honorary Doctorate of Sacred Theology at Northwestern's Commencement in June. Commencement at Northwestern is a time of celebration of the accomplishments of Northwestern's graduating students and their families. In light of the controversy around Dr. Wright and to ensure that the celebratory character of Commencement not be affected, the University has withdrawn its invitation to Dr. Wright. He was quoted as saying that his invitation to receive an honorary degree was withdrawn by Northwestern President Henry Bienen because Dr. Wright 'wasn't patriotic enough.' If Dr. Wright was quoted accurately, that statement is not true. In his conversation and correspondence with Dr. Wright in March, President Bienen never characterized Dr. Wright's views or made a judgment about them. The letter said, 'In light of the controversy surrounding statements made by you that have recently been publicized, the celebratory character of Northwestern's commencement would be affected by our conferring of this honorary degree. Thus I am withdrawing the offer of an honorary degree previously extended to you.' "

Images of the disaster in New Orleans and its aftermath had by now completely disappeared from the media, but any politician with a conscience, let alone progressive ideas, would not have forgotten what New Orleans had revealed to the shocked citizens of the East and West coasts: a third-world sector in the heart of the United States. That natural disasters are required to provide Americans with a glimpse of reality in their own country is an indication of the deep rot infecting the official political culture.

Obama's desire to appear "reasonable" to white America led him to forget things he'd learned nearer home. Research carried out by the Chicago Urban League on race and class imbalances in his native city would hardly have come as a surprise to him. He prided himself on his deep knowledge of sociology and politics on a local and a national level. The study's depressing figures revealed that economic and political discrimination reigned supreme in the heartland of "yes, we can" politics. Black household income overall was 58 percent that of white household income; 25 percent of Chicago's African American families were poor, compared to 5.6 percent of white families; 16 percent of Chicago's African Americans were categorized as living in "deep poverty," a group that included a third of the metropolitan area's black children; 94 percent of what the League characterized as the most poverty-stricken neighborhoods were predominantly African American. The situation was no better balanced in the upper reaches of Chicago society. Hardly surprising that 93 percent of the cash donated to the political campaigns came from largely white zones of relative affluence.[7] Corporate Chicago had embraced Obama.

---

7   Cited in Paul Street's myth-destroying *Barack Obama and the Future of American Politics*, Boulder, CO, 2008. This book is a useful antidote to the gushing biographies that adorn many a table in the chain bookstores.

So had Chicago's African American population. That combination helped propel him to power, arousing the jealousy of political rivals within his own party and a bitter, irrational hatred on the part of right-wing Republicans and nutty Libertarians.

From the very beginning Obama projected a desperate and passionate sincerity to become president. All the arts of political manipulation and prudent diplomacy of which his intellect was capable were brought into play to ensure success. Simultaneously timorous and wily, he presented himself as a politician who could unite the country, and flattering references to Ronald Reagan were not uncommon in his speeches and TV appearances. In one such interview he explained the importance of Reagan, who like himself opposed "excesses":

> I don't want to present myself as some sort of singular figure. I think part of what's different are the times. I do think that for example 1980 was different. I think Ronald Reagan changed the trajectory of America in a way that Richard Nixon did not and in a way that Bill Clinton did not. He put us on a fundamentally different path because the country was ready for it. I think they felt like with all the excesses of the 1960s and 1970s and government had grown and grown but there wasn't much sense of accountability in terms of how it was operating. I think people, he just tapped into what people were already feeling, which was we want clarity, we want optimism, we want a return to that sense of dynamism and entrepreneurship that had been missing.[8]

His campaign undoubtedly generated a new feeling of confidence, and the hopes of poor Chicagoans that this man would be able to protect them from the worst that society could throw at them

8 Video address to the *Reno Gazette* editorial board, January 14, 2008.

began to grow, and came to be shared by swathes of the African American citizens throughout the country. For some it was sufficient to just this once get a black family into the White House. African American historical memory may suffer the odd lapse, but it never disappears, and the figures cited above help to explain why this is so. They remember that slaves built the White House; that Frederick Douglass was denied entry to the same for Lincoln's second inauguration, lest a black face mar the celebrations; that Eleanor Roosevelt was constantly assailed by the press for regularly inviting African American leaders to tea at the mansion; that neither John Kennedy nor Lyndon Johnson ever invited Martin Luther King, Jr. to stay there; that till Clinton's presidency no black politician had spent a single night there as a guest. And now the First Lady was a direct descendant of slaves. The emblematic significance of Obama's victory should not be underestimated, but did it ever move beyond symbols?

A few perceptive African American scholars and activists who warned that it might not were voices in the wilderness. Adolph Reed, in particular, sought to explain that black politics was in decline and that the new breed of black politician was every bit as opportunistic as his white counterparts. Condoleezza Rice, Colin Powell and Clarence Thomas worked for the Republicans and had risen to occupy leading positions in state and government. Why should African American Democrats be left behind? As early as 1996, Reed mapped the path they were likely to take:

> In Chicago, for instance, we've gotten a foretaste of the new breed of foundation-hatched black communitarian voices; one of them, a smooth Harvard lawyer with impeccable do-good credentials and vacuous-to-repressive neoliberal politics, has won a state senate seat built on a base in the liberal foundation

and development worlds. His fundamentally bootstrap line was softened by a patina of the rhetoric of the authentic community, talk about meeting in kitchens, small-scale solutions to huge social problems, and the predictable elevation of process over program—the point where identity politics converges with old middle-class reform in favoring form over substance. I suspect that his ilk is the wave of the future in US black politics.[9]

Twelve years later, as Obama was busy fighting Hillary Clinton for the Democratic nomination, Reed reiterated his critique but lessened its impact considerably by declaring for Hillary Clinton:

He's a vacuous opportunist. I've never been an Obama supporter. I've known him since the very beginning of his political career, which was his campaign for the seat in my state senate district in Chicago. He struck me then as a vacuous opportunist, a good performer with an ear for how to make white liberals like him. I argued at the time that his fundamental political center of gravity, beneath an empty rhetoric of hope and change and new directions, is neoliberal.

His political repertoire has always included the repugnant stratagem of using connection with black audiences in exactly the same way Bill Clinton did—i.e., getting props both for emoting with the black crowd and talking through them to affirm a victim-blaming "tough love" message that focuses on alleged behavioral pathologies in poor black communities. Because he's able to claim racial insider standing, he actually goes beyond Clinton and rehearses the scurrilous and ridiculous sort of narrative Bill Cosby has made infamous.[10]

Reed was joined by Houston A. Baker, who castigated the treason of liberal, Ivy League–based black intellectuals and their neo-conservative cousins embedded in the Hoover Institute at

9 Adolph Reed, "The Curse of Community," *Village Voice*, January 16, 1996.
10 Adolph Reed, "Obama No," *Progressive*, May 2008.

Stanford, but by now the world had undergone a huge transformation. The trend so trenchantly criticized by Baker was, alas, universal. It did not simply apply to African Americans.

The Civil Rights movement is now taken for granted and retrospectively backed by most of the political mainstream. Obama and his hagiographers use it a great deal in explaining the intellectual and political formation of the new president. The struggle against segregation in Alabama and Mississippi is now deployed as a pleasing specter from the past, a ghostly presence ritually recalled on Martin Luther King, Jr. Day each year. Claiming King's mantle is all part of a day's work for Democrats, black and white and every other stripe, helping to create the impression that all good, thinking people once supported the struggle for black rights and desegregation. This was never the case. At virtually every level of the republic, the political culture of slavery continued to permeate most of its institutions. At its 1964 convention, to take but one instance, the Democratic Party refused to seat the pro–Civil Rights representatives from the Mississippi Freedom Democratic Party, preferring instead to back the segregationists representing the lynch mobs. Hardly surprising that many young black activists in those days imbibed the slogan "Never trust a white liberal" at an early age. Denied entry to the universe of mainstream politics and a great deal else, African Americans decided to fight back. It was civil disobedience that won them civil rights.

Martin Luther King, Jr. never believed that the final victories had been won. For him, "the Negro still lives in the basement of the Great Society." The Civil Rights movement had achieved a great deal, but more was needed. He did more. He educated his supporters in the economic and political realities of the time. This fact explains the sharp rise in black political consciousness in the ghettoes and the basements. His frequent statements on the class divide between rich and poor sound almost utopian today. His denunciation of US foreign policy was couched in language not dissimilar to that used by the much maligned Pastor Wright. It was King, after all, who once said, "The greatest purveyor of violence in the world is my own country." In "Where Do We Go From Here?" a prescient speech warning against complacency and delivered a year before he was killed, King spoke clearly and to the point. He could do this because he had something to say:

> In short, over the last ten years the Negro decided to straighten his back up, realizing that a man cannot ride your back unless it is bent. We made our government write new laws to alter some of the cruelest injustices that affected us. We made an indifferent and unconcerned nation rise from lethargy and subpoenaed its conscience to appear before the judgment seat of morality on the whole question of civil rights. We gained manhood in the nation that had always called us "boy." … But in spite of a decade of significant progress, the problem is far from solved. The deep rumbling of discontent in our cities is indicative of the fact that the plant of freedom has grown only a bud and not yet a flower …
>
> He is still at the bottom, despite the few who have penetrated to slightly higher levels. Even where the door has been forced partially open, mobility for the Negro is still sharply restricted. There is often no bottom at which to start, and when there is, there's almost no room at the top. In consequence, Negroes are still impoverished aliens in an affluent society. They are too poor even to rise with the society, too impoverished by the ages to be able to ascend by using their own resources. And the Negro did not do this himself; it was done to him. For more than half of his American history, he was enslaved. Yet, he built the spanning bridges and the grand mansions, the sturdy docks and stout factories of the South. His

unpaid labor made cotton "King" and established America as a significant nation in international commerce. Even after his release from chattel slavery, the nation grew over him, submerging him. It became the richest, most powerful society in the history of man, but it left the Negro far behind.[11]

King ended his speech by linking the costs of an ugly, escalating war in Vietnam—a war in which a disproportionately high number of blacks fought and died—to the social problems at home:

And I say to you today, that if our nation can spend thirty-five billion dollars a year to fight an unjust, evil war in Vietnam, and twenty billion dollars to put a man on the moon, it can spend billions of dollars to put God's children on their own two feet right here on earth.[12]

Stokely Carmichael, one of the founders of SNCC (Student Nonviolent Coordinating Committee), changed his ideas after numerous activists were beaten to a pulp or, in some cases, killed by the Ku Klux Klan and racist police outfits linked to them. His slogan, "Black Power," he once told me during a break in the 1967 Dialectics of Liberation conference in London, was designed to free black people from a deeply ingrained sense of inferiority, the result of slavery and post-slavery subjugation. Unless this happened it would be impossible for African Americans to play any equal role in united struggles with white radicals in the United States. He had noticed that in SNCC, and the experience had seared him. Earlier, the Trinidadian historian C. L. R. James had

11   Dr. Martin Luther King, Jr., "Where Do We Go from Here?" Available online at stanford.edu.
12   Ibid.

lambasted him in public for this slogan and denounced it as "frivo-
lous" and "non-Marxist." Carmichael had laughed and shouted,
"You're out of touch, old man." Later, he confided that he was
a great fan of James and that his idea of "Black Power" had, in
fact, grown out of reading *The Black Jacobins* and other books.
I told him I agreed with James. Our conversation soon ended.
Carmichael's trajectory was the reverse of other militants in that
period. He had started his political work in an organization that
united black and white students. Some of the latter had also suffered martyrdom, killed by the same set of gangsters who burned
black people. He preferred to work among his own, criticizing
those who did otherwise.

Malcolm X, on the other hand, had started his political life in
the Nation of Islam, realized its insufficiencies and moved on to
demand a just society both racially and economically and, most
importantly, stated in public that only an integrated struggle of
blacks and whites could achieve such a goal. And, understanding
that integration had to take place on every level, he defended
mixed marriages, angering both the Nation of Islam and the White
Nation supremacists, many of whom were embedded in the
politics and coercive agencies of the country.

Carmichael fled the country and settled in the African Republic
of Guinea. Malcolm X, as he had predicted, was assassinated by
killers dispatched by the Nation of Islam, possibly acting in concert
with the FBI. Many of the facts remain hidden from public view.
Martin Luther King, Jr. denounced US violence in Vietnam and
elsewhere in extremely sharp language and announced his decision
to stand as an independent peace candidate (with Dr. Benjamin
Spock as his VP) against the Democratic incumbent. He, too, was
assassinated in full public view, on April 4, 1968. It has been

alleged that the state was secretly involved and the circumstantial evidence in favor of this view makes for interesting reading.[13] Two days later the country was on fire—literally. Federal troops were dispatched to occupy twenty-one cities, including Washington, DC. In some seventy-two cities the police were waging war on the black ghettoes. In some cases they tried to provoke young African Americans to enter the streets where they could be tear-gassed, shot and arrested. The Black Panther leaders warned against provocateurs and told the angry youth that revolutions were not made by throwing rocks and bottles, and their prestige was such that they succeeded in preventing a number of massacres.

Subsequently, the Black Panther Party leadership was also targeted and many of its leaders were killed or given lengthy prison sentences. The BPP was the first serious attempt since the Civil War to organize black people around a political program coupled with self-defense. The image of disciplined and armed groups of black men and women, politically motivated and completely dedicated to their cause, marching in black berets through the streets of San Francisco, New York and Chicago did strike fear into the establishment. It was not the weapons that worried them, but the threat of the potential power they were acquiring and actual influence they wielded over the new generation of African Americans.

The origins and development of the BPP are interesting and not without some indirect relevance to the subject of this book. The Black Panthers began life in 1965 as a monitoring organization dedicated to protecting African Americans from random arrests, searches and brutalities—part of everyday life in Oakland

---

13   William Pepper, *An Act of State: The Execution of Martin Luther King*, London, 2003.

then and now—by recording all instances of such activities. They were unapologetic in the defense of black human rights, deliberately provocative in the language they used, and active in defending their constitutional right to bear arms, a right the police did not respect in the case of black people. The Panthers were proud of being viewed as "uppity niggers." J. Edgar Hoover, the FBI dictator, a closet homosexual,[14] declared that the Panthers were "the greatest internal threat to the internal security of the country." US Attorney-General John Mitchell (forced to resign during the Watergate scandal) promised that the Justice Department "would wipe out the Black Panther Party by the end of 1969."[15]

The Oakland police embarked on a systematic campaign of persecution that included arrests, other forms of harassment, and shoot-outs. The Panthers shot back when attacked, challenging the monopoly of legitimate violence enjoyed by the authorities. When asked about the cult of violence that surrounded the Panthers, Bobby Seale replied:

> It was never the intention of the Panthers to police the streets of West Oakland by our own force of arms. We just wanted to let the brothers on the block find out what was happening. We are saying that we want every black brother to put a shotgun in his

14   The only reason to mention his sexual orientation is because of the utter hypocrisy that accompanied it: Hoover publicly declared his strong belief in "family values" and his hostility to "perverts," etc. Some months before he died of AIDS, the filmmaker Derek Jarman and I were discussing a script based on a Géricault painting, *The Raft of the Medusa*, in which all those on the raft were AIDS victims. A posthumous biography of Hoover had detailed his secret life. I suggested that it might be an idea to lighten the load by having the filming interrupted by the entry of forties-style G-men and Hoover stepping out of a black limo attired in a glittering red dress and earrings. We laughed at various versions of this and a script was being written when Derek died.
15   *Newsweek*, February 19, 1969.

house. We are saying that's necessary. We are saying we need to protect ourselves against police protection. That's all.

Like Malcolm X before them, Eldridge Cleaver and Huey Newton, the principal Panther strategists, realized that black liberation could never be achieved in isolation from progressives in the white communities. Close links were soon established with the Peace and Freedom Party. Neither group was large, but it was not inconceivable at the time that the combination could become more powerful and constitute a powerful bloc of dissidents on a national scale. As in the case of Malcolm X, once the Panthers had moved in this direction the police and FBI decided that the brutes had to be politically and, where necessary, physically exterminated. This meant infiltrating their ranks and executing their leaders without mercy. Official inquiries of a surreal nature were instituted to ascertain whether the civil rights of the Panthers had been violated. One can imagine a question and answer session not revealed to the public:

Q: Officer X, were you aware that when you shot Black Panther Bobby Hutton dead you were violating his civil rights?
A: No, sir. I was not aware of that fact.

The Oakland police killed Hutton in 1968. Eldridge Cleaver, who was with him at the time, survived only because too many people were watching, and having seen young Bobby gunned down they started yelling and cursing when the Oakland cops turned their guns on Cleaver, who had walked out of the building naked, except for his socks, just to show he wasn't carrying any weapons. Fred Hampton was executed in Chicago; FBI hirelings in Los Angeles assassinated Al Carter and John Higgins in 1969; George

Jackson was murdered in San Quentin prison in 1971. Cleaver went into exile in Algeria for a while, returning to find an unrecognizable landscape. He drifted for a while and then found comfort in the deity and Ronald Reagan. He was the only major Panther leader (if not the only contributor to *Ramparts* magazine) who executed such an abrupt about-face: the author of *Soul on Ice* became a small businessman and a born-again Christian, flirted with Mormonism, and subsequently joined the Republican Party in the 1980s. He died in 1998. Be killed or be co-opted was the choice that Panthers were offered, but few deserted to the Republicans. Many became Democrats.

Bobby Seale, a former US Air Force pilot who had been court-martialed for disobeying a racist senior officer, and the author of the mesmerizing *Seize the Time* managed to survive prison. On his release, he realized that the party had been decimated. He decided to retire from active politics, but he never denounced or regretted his past.

Huey Newton continued to carry the flame, turning to the academy and producing a penetrating analysis of the Black Panther experience. His story is revelatory of much that typified the San Francisco Bay Area in that period. In October 1967, Newton was stopped by an Oakland police officer, who attempted to disarm him. Another policeman arrived and shots were exchanged. Newton was seriously wounded and arrested. He then lost consciousness. A policeman was killed and another slightly injured. The injured police officer told the court that the firing began after Newton had been arrested and disarmed. The most likely scenario is that the cops fired at each other, either deliberately or accidentally. The unconscious Newton was taken to Kaiser Hospital and woke to find himself with four bullets in his abdomen and one in his thigh. Here, in agony and visibly bleeding, he was greeted by Miss Corrine Leonard, a white nurse, who pelted him with a list of questions. She later testified at his trial:

> I heard a moaning and a groaning and I went over and this Negro fellow was there. I asked him if he belonged to Kaiser and he said, "Yes, yes. Can't you see I'm bleeding? C'mon, get a doctor out here," and I asked him if he had his Kaiser card, and he got quite upset at this and said, "I've been shot," and I said, "I see this, but you are not in acute distress."

Half an hour later a doctor arrived but refused to treat Newton till the police were present to manacle him and strap him to the operating table. This was done, and took more time. Newton was photographed in this posture. At least one senior surgeon, Dr. Mary Jane Aguilar, would later protest in a letter to the local paper, writing that she could not recall anything in her medical training suggesting that "acute abdominal injury, severe pain and hemorrhaging are best treated by manacling the patient to the examining table in such a way that the back is arched and the belly tense."

Despite the best efforts of the hospital, Newton survived. Despite the conflicting evidence (not dissimilar to that in the case of former Black Panther Mumia Abu-Jamal, currently on death row in Philadelphia), he was convicted by a grand jury in Alameda County in exactly twenty-seven minutes. The defense lawyer, Charles Garry, maintained that no black person accused of killing a policeman could ever get a fair trial in the county or, he could have added, in the country as a whole. In September 1968, Newton was charged with "voluntary manslaughter," convicted, and sentenced to two to fifteen years in prison. In May 1970, the

California Appellate Court accepted what most lawyers already knew: the trial had been so full of flaws that there should never have been a conviction in the first place. It was overturned. After two more mistrials, the State of California dropped all charges. Mumia Abu-Jamal has been less fortunate.

Newton devoted himself solidly to intellectual labors at University of California, Santa Cruz, but never reneged on his beliefs. On August 22, 1989, he was shot dead in West Oakland by Tyrone Robinson, a young black drug dealer masquerading as a member of some fantasy "revolutionary organization" either set up or heavily infiltrated by the FBI. Robinson claimed he had fired in self-defense, but the police found no evidence that Newton had been armed. In fact, like the assassination of Malcolm X, this one had been planned. Just before he was executed with three bullets to his head Newton calmly told his killer: "You can kill my body, but you can't kill my soul. My soul will live forever!"

There are many footnotes to the Panther legacy. One of them concerns Chicago's South Side. Here Bobby Rush, the deputy minister of defense of the Illinois chapter of the Black Panther Party, had, after the demise of the organization and most of its leaders, decided to join the African American caucus in the Democratic Party and was elected to the Chicago City Council in the 1980s. He backed Harold Washington for mayor in a campaign polarized by race. Washington won. Rush prospered and was elected a congressman in 1993. Seven years later he took on Richard M. Daley in the mayoral election in Chicago and lost. Daley, never one to forget a slight, decided that one of the young terriers in the state senate should be tested. He encouraged, to put it at its mildest, the man with the lean and hungry look to challenge Rush in the primaries in 2000.[16] Obama was thrashed and Rush gloated:

> Barack was just no threat. The forces that created him were the same forces that were always coming after me ... Barack was backed by the liberal elite cadre or cabal that came out of Hyde Park. These folks, they didn't like me. I'm not Harvard or Ivy League ... I wasn't upper crust. I'm a former Black Panther.[17]

Rush was equally contemptuous of the way in which Obama carefully constructed his new image for the South Side and its equivalents elsewhere in the land:

> "It's amazing how he formed a black identity," Rush said, rising from his desk and starting, theatrically, to sashay across his office, mimicking Obama's sinuous walk. "Barack's walk is an adaptation of a strut that comes from the street. There's a

16   "Obama's brash self-confidence led him into his only big political blunder. Prodded by the Daley machine, he challenged Bobby Rush, an incumbent Democratic congressman and former Black Panther, in 2000. Rush pounded Obama by more than 2 to 1 in the primary. 'He was blinded by his ambition,' Rush told the *New York Times* last year." "Obama: A Thin Record for a Bridge Builder," *Washington Post*, March 2, 2008. Was it a political blunder? I don't think so. It was blind ambition that led him to become an instrument of the Daley machine, an apparatus as effective and as corrupt but even less tolerant of dissent inside Democrat-controlled institutions than was the current mayor's late father, Richard J. Daley. The two big books on Obama by David Remnick and Jonathan Alter either ignore Obama's links to the Daley machine or, in the case of Alter, insist that "Obama was never a real part of the Daley machine." (Jonathan Alter, *The Promise: President Obama, Year One*, New York, 2010, 25) Was he then a virtual, unreal or surreal part of the Daley family apparatus patiently and carefully built up over the past sixty years? We need to be told. The notion that he could have won Illinois and the nomination without the central involvement of the Chicago machine and its cogs is risible.
17   David Remnick, *The Bridge*, New York, 2010. Pages 307–33 provide an interesting account of how the Black Panthers were infiltrated, Fred Hampton's killing by the Chicago police, and Bobby Rush's surrender to the police in the presence of five hundred activists and Jesse Jackson.

certain break at the knees as you walk and you get a certain *roll*
going. Watch. You see?" Rush laughed at his own imitation.
"And he's the first president of the United States to walk like
that, I can guarantee you that! But lemme tell you, I never
noticed that he walked like that *back then*."[18]

The triumph of capitalism in the late twentieth century had led
many European and white North American radicals to change
sides; it would have been a miracle had the bulk of their African
American counterparts remained steadfast. The trend had been
visible much earlier. It was Ronald Reagan, after all, who first
offered a senior position to a former Black Panther supporter from
a poor family, Clarence Thomas, and it was Bush senior who
appointed Thomas to the Supreme Court. His son George W.
Bush appointed a neocon African American, Condoleezza Rice,
as his national security adviser, and a black general, Colin Powell,
served as his secretary of state. The leap from this to Obama was
not as great as some imagined. The symbolic significance, however, was such that even Ms. Rice had moist eyes when the
Obama family entered the big house on Pennsylvania Avenue.
This unprecedented event in US history excited many parts of
the world, especially Europe, desperate for an American leader
it could follow without embarrassment. It was automatically
assumed that the new leader of the world's only imperial state
would heal the wounds of the past. Some of the victims of
Hurricane Katrina in Louisiana, members of Operation Enduring
Freedom in Afghanistan, and people living in occupied Iraq and
Palestine, as well as citizens of the European protectorate, injected
themselves with hope. This time it might be different.[19]

18   Ibid.
19   And not just them. I was saddened to read Manning Marable's essay "African

But underlying all of this was a democratic system that appeared to have exhausted its historical function. Tocqueville used to argue that history revealed an irresistible forward movement in the direction of a much greater "equality of conditions." He articulated this view of history in the opening pages of *Democracy in America*:

> The gradual trend towards equality of conditions is a fact of Providence, of which it bears the principal characteristics: it is universal, it is enduring, it constantly eludes human powers of control; all events and all men contribute to its development. Would it be wise to think that a social movement of such remote origin can be suspended by the efforts of one generation? Can it be supposed that democracy, after destroying feudalism and overwhelming kings, will yield before the powers of money and business—*devant les bourgeois et les riches*?

He got it slightly wrong. It was not democracy but revolutions and civil wars of one sort or another, usually backed by wealthy merchants, active philosophers and armed peasants that ended feudal absolutism. Democracy in the meaningful sense of the word was instituted gradually and in its fullest sense only after the First World War when women won the right to vote. In the United States, the descendants of slaves had to struggle for another four decades, endure numerous hardships and make more sacrifices before they were finally able to register and vote in many Southern states. In his PhD dissertation, Huey Newton referred to two key obstacles that retarded the development of democracy from the very beginning:

American Peacemakers: Dr. Martin Luther King, Jr., Barack Obama and the Struggle Against Racism, Inequality and War," *Black Commentator*, April 10, 2008. I have enormous respect for much of Marable's previous work, but this was little more than sentimental illusion-mongering, as has become obvious since.

1. Class and racial cleavages which have historically been the source of division and bitter antagonism between sectors of American society; and

2. The inherent and longstanding distrust held by the American ruling class of any institutionalized democracy involving the mass of the population.[20]

In the meantime, American democracy was bending the knee to corporate wealth. The merger of politics and money that once was able to circumvent the electoral process has now absorbed it. Centuries ago, both Shakespeare and Goethe warned of the power of gold, its capacity to disrupt and corrupt. Shakespeare used the antique world to illustrate a universal truth by writing these lines for a sad and disillusioned Timon of Athens:

> Gold? Yellow, glittering precious gold? No, gods,
> I am no idle votarist: roots, you clear heavens!
> Thus much of this will make black, white; foul, fair;
> Wrong, right; base, noble; old, young; coward, valiant;
> … This yellow slave
> Will knit and break religions; bless th' accurst;
> Make the hoar leprosy adored; place thieves,
> And give them title, knee, and approbation,
> With senators on the bench![21]

The symbiosis between big money and big politics was visible in most parts of the world, but in the United States money had become a visible Godhead; its influence had reached an astonishing level, reducing politics to public relations, institutionalizing apathy and often consigning creativity, boldness and intellectual

20   Huey Newton, "War Against the Panthers: A Study of Repression in America," University of California, Santa Cruz, 1980.
21   William Shakespeare, *Timon of Athens*, act 4, sc. 3, 26–9, 33–7.

experimentation to the dustbin. Underneath the harmonizing plu-
ralism lay the dictatorship of capital. All pretence disappeared after
the collapse of the old communist enemy. What could not be
done before was now possible through money. From his Princeton perch the political theorist Sheldon S. Wolin mapped the
decline of accountability in American politics over many decades.
For him it is a "fugitive democracy" in which the corruptions of
empire and the stranglehold of the corporations have created a
system that has killed any meaningful democratic activity, and "so
integral are lobbyists to the legislative process that they have been
known to write legislative bills for congressmen and senators and
enjoy use of congressional office space." Wolin's gloomy, but
accurate, view of the country's drift away from democracy was
given a surprising boost by the January 2010 Supreme Court decision in *Citizens United* v. *FEC*. In the name of "freedom of
speech" as guaranteed by the first amendment, five right-wing jus-
tices declared on their own initiative that corporations and their
lobbyists could spend as much cash as they liked to fund TV com-
mercials in support of their favored candidates. Obama was not
pleased. His expression of dissent revealed an unusual intensity,
not to mention a breach of his consensual style of politics, even
though it could be argued that the judges were simply making
transparent and taking to its logical conclusion a mechanism that
was firmly in place. This presidential pique might have been mar-
ginally more effective had he stuck to an earlier pledge and
restricted his campaign spending, as his Republican opponent
wanted. Nor did a publicly funded presidential system require any
new legislation. It already existed. Instead Obama chose corporate
cash, and spun the small donations as an "alternative public-
finance system." Faced with clear choices, he went for the worst,

but pretended to have done otherwise, a pattern that, after his victory, he would soon establish in most other spheres.

Obama raised more money—most of it, contrary to campaign mythology, in large corporate donations—than Hillary Clinton before and during the primaries, and much more than his Republican rival during the actual campaign. The donors included some of Wall Street's finest, investing in their futures: Goldman Sachs ($994,795), Microsoft ($833,617), UBS AG ($543,219), Lehman Brothers, in 2007 ($318,467), JPMorgan Chase ($695,132). There were also substantial donations from Time-Warner, IBM, Morgan Stanley, General Electric, Exxon, Google; three top-drawer law firms coughed up $15.8 million. Stanford and Columbia Universities sent checks for half a million each, and the University of California sent a million and a half on its own. Practical self-interest dictated that the bulging coffers (he had raised a total of $900 million) of the Obama campaign be used to pay off a large chunk of Senator Clinton's debts. Once she was promised what she required, she signed a truce with her rival. Was the ink indelible?

This devil's bargain with big business was leavened by the constant invocation of the deity in most of Obama's speeches, not as inappropriately as some might think. Any imperial president can always do with some extraterrestrial help. He would only be following in the footsteps of the first settler families. A traditional story related of the early settlers in Milford, Connecticut, tells how they were temporarily overcome by a crisis of conscience. Should they be stealing all the Native Americans' land? The scriptures were summoned and closely scrutinized, that the settlers might fully understand the divine plan. After a brief discussion the colonists decided that:

1. The earth is the Lord's and the fullness thereof. Voted.
2. The Lord can dispose of the earth to his saints. Voted.
3. We are his saints. Voted.

Till now, Obama's presidency has been distinguished largely by the way it has continued on the course established by his recent predecessors. Despite the severity of the economic crisis and the disastrous wars abroad, the consensus holds. Obama is little more than the Empire's most inventive apparition of itself. The fact that even this is unacceptable to the most extreme defenders of the imperial project can be seen or heard most nights on Fox television and right-wing radio, where these venues' shallow, coarse and swaggering rabble regularly present Obama as a "socialist" who is soft on Islam, not sufficiently pro-Israel, and may not have been born in the United States and therefore may even be an "illegal president" but in any case certainly remains an out-of-control radical. If only. None of the right-wing hysteria bears any relation to reality.

The portrayal of Obama as a good man in a bad world is no more convincing. The argument that compromises are sometimes essential to achieve limited progressive aims is correct. The problem is that Obama, while an extremely intelligent human being, is not a progressive leader by any stretch of the imagination. Wishing that he were is fine but does not bring about the required transformation.

In reality, Barack Obama is a skillful and gifted machine politician who rapidly rose to the top. Once that is understood there is little about him that should surprise anyone: to talk of betrayal is foolish, for nothing has been betrayed but one's own illusions. A fellow Democrat in Chicago sums it all up quite well:

I first met Barack Obama about 14 years ago. He was a young lawyer, a state representative preparing to run for Congress, and also a guy many saw as a rising star. In fact, it was not long after that first meeting that he and I began our climb up the political ladder in Chicago that would one day make me governor of the state, and on this day, make him president of our country … moments after the new president took his oath of office, I was at the federal courthouse in downtown Chicago getting finger-printed by a deputy US marshal … He's now president of the United States, like Zeus in Greek mythology, on top of Mount Olympus. I'm Icarus, who flew too close to the sun. And I crashed to the ground.[22]

Some win, others lose.

Is Michelle Obama, the first direct descendant of slaves to become First Lady, a winner or a loser? Opinions vary. Eleanor Roosevelt often embarrassed her husband by her radical affiliations and her outspoken views on a number of questions, and it was her uncompromising hostility to segregation that created the most controversy. She refused to pander to popular prejudices. Hillary Clinton, when she occupied the same position, retained a strong interest in political issues and was not shy about speaking up for a better health care system before she and Bill caved in to the insurance companies and their friends in Senate and House. Michelle Obama, as we know, is an intelligent woman. What explains the cause she has chosen, her obesity obsession? If she is serious then she will know what is required: structural changes in the production and distribution of food in public institutions and elsewhere. Till now she has tended in the direction of treating it as an individual problem. Parents rather than poverty. Individual indiscipline rather than the food industry.

22   Rod Blagojevich, *The Governor*, Los Angeles, 2009.

During the last fifty years the physical image of the prosperous and the poor in the United States has been turned upside down. From the Gilded Age to the close of the Belle Epoque in Europe, political cartoons contrasted obscenely corpulent millionaires with the skeletal poor, and novels described the agonies suffered by rich men with gout. Today, slim-line CEOs and Hollywood elite are advertising icons for the body beautiful, gout is a disease of poor people, and obesity increasingly an affliction of poor children.

The reason has little to do with careless parenting or individual weakness—a view monotonously peddled by Mrs. Obama and reminiscent of her husband at his worst—but is the direct consequence of the disturbing symbiosis between politicians and global corporations. Giant food and facility industries operate cafeterias in schools, hospitals, universities and military facilities. They buy from suppliers who provide kickbacks and cut corners to keep profits stable, not those who provide healthy food choices.[23]

The pernicious effect of TV advertising that uses popular cartoon characters has also been noted by researchers: "We now have clear evidence of something many people suspected—that the use of these licensed characters has an impact on children's preferences in food," says Dr. Thomas Robinson, director of the Center for Healthy Weight at Stanford University's School of Medicine. "People want to blame the parents, but the parents don't have billions of dollars to spend on counter-advertising."[24]

23 During a fortnight I spent in Flint, Michigan, in 2009, a despairing teacher confided that some of the young children in her class were so overweight that they could not sit on the floor, since standing up again was too much of an effort. She, at least, understood that only a sharp shift in social priorities on a federal level could bring about any change.

24 Dierdre Lockwood, "Shrek Lures Kids to Sugary Snacks," *Chicago Tribune*, June 21, 2010.

Michelle Obama's "Let's Move" campaign is unlikely to take on the manufacturers' lobby short of a huge scandal/disaster involving food poisoning and children. Even then, I fear, the aim would be damage limitation. In the meantime, instead of mimicking workout hostesses on breakfast TV, she could pressure her husband and his colleagues on Capitol Hill to regulate the production of children's food and ban the use of licensed TV characters to promote junk. That would be a healthy start.

2

PRESIDENT OF CANT

Two years since the White House changed hands, how has the American empire altered? Under the Bush administration it was widely believed, in both mainstream opinion and much of the amnesiac section of the left, that the United States had fallen under an aberrant regime, the product of a virtual coup d'état by a coterie of right-wing fanatics—alternatively, ultra-reactionary corporations—who had hijacked American democracy for policies of unprecedented aggression in the Middle East. In reaction, the election to the presidency of a mixed-race Democrat who vowed to heal America's wounds at home and restore its reputation abroad was greeted with a wave of ideological euphoria not seen since the days of Kennedy. Once again, America could show its true face—purposeful but peaceful; firm but generous; humane, respectful, multicultural—to the world. Naturally, with the makings of a Lincoln or a Roosevelt for our time in him, the country's new young ruler would have to make compromises, as any statesman must. But at least the shameful interlude of Republican swagger and criminality was over. Bush and Cheney had broken the continuity of a multilateral American leadership that had served the country well throughout the Cold War and after. Obama would now restore it.

Rarely has self-interested mythology—or well-meaning gull-ibility—been more quickly exposed. There was no fundamental break in foreign policy, as opposed to diplomatic mood music, between the Bush One, Clinton, and Bush Two administrations; there has been none between the Bush and Obama regimes. The strategic goals and imperatives of the US imperium remain the same, as do its principal theaters and means of operation. Even before the collapse of the USSR, the Carter Doctrine—the construction of another democratic pillar of human rights—had defined the greater Middle East as the central battlefield for the imposition of American power around the world. It is enough to look at each of its sectors to see that Obama is the offspring of Bush, as Bush the son was of Clinton and Clinton of Bush the father, as so many appropriately biblical begettings.

Obama's line toward Israel would be manifest even before he took office. On December 27, 2008, the Israeli Defense Force launched an all-out air and ground assault on the population of Gaza. Bombing, burning, killing continued without interruption for twenty-two days, during which time the president-elect uttered not a syllable of reproof. By prearrangement, Tel Aviv called off its blitz shortly before his inauguration on January 20, 2009, not to spoil the party. By then Obama had picked the ultra-Zionist Doberman from Chicago, Rahm Emanuel, a former volunteer for the IDF, as his chief of staff. Once installed, Obama, like every US president, called for peace between the two suffering peoples of the Holy Land, and again, like every predecessor, for Palestinians to recognize Israel and for Israel to stop building settlements in the territories it seized in 1967. Within a week of the president's speech in Cairo pledging opposition to further settlements, the

Netanyahu coalition was extending Jewish properties in East Jerusalem with impunity. By the autumn, Secretary of State Clinton was congratulating Netanyahu on the "unprecedented concessions" his government had made. She was asked by Mark Landler of the *New York Times*, at a press conference in Jerusalem, "Madame Secretary, when you were here in March on the first visit, you issued a strong statement condemning the demolition of housing units in East Jerusalem. Yet, that demolition has continued unabated, and indeed, a few days ago, the mayor of the city of Jerusalem issued a new order for demolition. How would you characterize this policy today?" She did not deign to reply.[1]

A month earlier, the UN fact-finding mission set up to look at the invasion of Gaza had reported that the IDF had not always acted by the book, though naturally rocket attacks by Hamas had provoked their actions. Chaired by one of the most notorious time-servers of "international justice," the South African judge Richard Goldstone, a prosecutor at the preorchestrated Hague Tribunal on Yugoslavia and a self-professed Zionist, the mission's complaints against Israel could hardly have been feebler, in startling contrast to the testimony they heard in Gaza, which was made available on their Web site.[2] Even so, unaccustomed to establishment criticism of any kind, Tel Aviv reacted with dudgeon, and so Washington instructed its client at the head of the

---

1 "Remarks with Israeli Prime Minister Binyamin Netanyahu," US Department of State, October 31, 2009 available online at www.state.gov.

2 In an interview with Israeli Army Radio conducted in Hebrew, Nicole Goldstone, the judge's daughter, said, "My father took on this job because he thought he is doing the best thing for peace, for everyone and also for Israel … It wasn't easy. My father did not expect to see and hear what he saw and heard." She told the radio station that had it not been for her father the report would have been harsher. One could add that had it not been for the presence on the mission of a feisty Pakistani woman lawyer, Hina Jilani, the report would have been even softer.

PLO, Mahmoud Abbas, that he must oppose any consideration of it at the UN.[3] This was too much even for Abbas's followers, and amid the ensuing uproar he had to retract, discrediting himself even further. The episode confirmed that the American Israel Public Affairs Committee's (AIPAC) grip on Washington remains as strong as ever—contrary to the delusions of some on the US left that the Israel lobby of old, never really much of a force, was now being superseded by a more enlightened brand of American Zionism.

In the Palestinian theater of the American system, the lack of any significant novelty does not imply lack of movement. Viewed from a longer perspective, US policy has for some time been to coax Israel toward the creation of one or more bantustans, in its own best interests.[4] The condition of that has, of course, been the elimination of any prospect of a genuine Palestinian leadership or real Palestinian state. The Oslo Accords were a first step in this process, destroying the credibility of the PLO by setting up a Palestinian Authority that was little more than a Potemkin façade for the real authority in the Occupied Territories, the IDF. Incapable of achieving even token independence, the PLO leadership in the West Bank settled down to make money, leaving the bulk of the Palestinian people helpless: mired in poverty and regularly subjected to settler violence. In contrast, by creating a primitive but effective welfare system, capable of distributing food and

---

3   The Israelis applied the ultimate sanction: if Abbas endorsed the Goldstone Report, the mobile phone deal between an Israeli company and senior PLO personnel was off.

4   Though it should be pointed out that both Bishop Tutu and Ronnie Kasrils, former deputy defense minister in the Mandela government, vehemently dispute the analogy. They insist that the condition of Palestinians in the occupied territories is far worse than was that of blacks in the bantustans.

medical care in poor neighborhoods and looking after the weak, Hamas was able to win enough popular support to triumph in the Palestinian elections of 2006. Euro-America reacted with an immediate political and economic boycott, hoisting Fatah back into power on the West Bank. In Gaza, where Hamas was strongest, Israel had for some time been inciting a coup by Mohammed Dahlan, Washington's favorite thug in the PLO security apparatus. Defense Minister Ben-Eliezer has openly testified before the Knesset Foreign Affairs and Defense Committee that in 2002, when the IDF pulled out of Gaza, he offered the Strip to Dahlan, who was quite willing to launch a Palestinian civil war, long a twinkle in the eye of many an Israeli colonizer. Four years later Dahlan was primed by Washington to implement a military putsch in Gaza, but was beaten to the punch by Hamas, which took over the Strip in mid 2007.[5] After Euro-American political and economic punishment of the voters for defying the West came Israeli military retribution, with the assault of late 2008, winked at by Obama and the European leaders.

But the result is not the impasse so regularly deplored by well-wishers of a "peaceful settlement." Under repeated blows, and amid increasing isolation, the Palestinian resistance is being gradually weakened to a point where Hamas itself—unable to develop any coherent strategy, or to break with the Oslo Accords of which it, too, has become a prisoner—is edging toward acceptance of the pittance on offer from Israel, garnished with a solatium from the West. No meaningful Palestinian Authority exists. Elected representatives from the West Bank or Gaza are treated like mendicant NGOs: rewarded if they remain on their knees and follow

5   See David Rose, "The Gaza Bombshell," *Vanity Fair*, April 2008.

Western bidding, sanctioned if they step out of line. Rationally, Palestinians would do far better to dissolve the Authority and insist on equal citizenship rights within a single state, backed by an international campaign for boycott, divestment and sanction till the apartheid structures of Israel are dismantled. Practically, there is little or no chance of this in the immediate future. In all probability what lies ahead is the convergence—already being hailed in *Haaretz* as even more enlightened than Rabin—of Obama and Netanyahu on a final solution of "Palestinian" entities Israel can live with, and Palestine can die in.

Netanyahu and Ehud Barak needed Obama to push through their plan. Obama needed them in order to get AIPAC and its network of supporters all over the country to back him in advance of the 2010 midterm elections. Pro-Israel money plays a significant role in US elections, and AIPAC's approval can be decisive where the race is close. There is only one criterion: blind loyalty to Israel and blind denunciation of those who are critical of its policies as bigots and anti-Semites. Candidates for the presidency, the House and the Senate from both parties queue obediently at AIPAC gatherings to pledge support and receive largesse.[6]

As often happens in this region, the best of plans laid by Israeli leaders and their Washington friends have gone awry. Netanyahu's visit to the White House, after a triumphant Canadian tour, was hurriedly cancelled in May 2010 after the Israeli leadership underestimated the impact of the Israeli military assault on a peaceful flotilla taking medicines, medical equipment and other humanitarian aid to the Palestinian ghetto. Nine Turkish peace activists were

6   For a detailed survey of the linkage between the Israel lobby and US politics, see Michael Massing, "The Storm over the Israel Lobby," *New York Review of Books*, June 8, 2008.

killed on board the Turkish vessel Mavi Marmara. Others were arrested and taken to Israel. Netanyahu and Ehud Barak had orchestrated and authorized the attack. They had underestimated the response.

Reaction in most parts of the world was outrage. Even the German government, usually crippled by Israel's cynical blackmail, was compelled to make some mild criticisms. Even as the British government called Israel's behavior "unacceptable" and demanded an immediate lifting of the siege, BBC television became an unfiltered vehicle for Israeli propaganda. Most of Europe echoed the British government view. Egypt was forced to open its frontier with Gaza, and even Mahmoud Abbas managed a few angry words. The United States refused to criticize Israeli actions, making a mockery of Turkey's membership in NATO, and privately vetoed any UN inquiry. Instead, Netanyahu was "pressured" to permit two "international observers," a Canadian judge and David Trimble from Ulster, to sit in as observers without vote on the internal inquiry agreed to by the Israeli cabinet. International law is not applicable to the United States. Now the entire world is aware that it doesn't apply to Israel either. What seemed like pure arrogance on the part of Israel's rulers might well have been selective punishment for Turkey, which had dared, together with Brazil, to defy US–Israeli pressures isolating and sanctioning Iran, and had begun to mediate independently to defuse the nuclear issue.

For the moment, however, despite the flotilla deaths, there are more pressing preoccupations than Palestine: war zones farther east have the first call on imperial attention. Iraq may have dropped from the headlines, but it hasn't from the daily security briefings in the Oval Office. In 2002, on his way up the political ladder as a low-profile state senator in Illinois, Obama opposed the attack on Iraq; it was politically inexpensive to do so. By the time he was elected president, American forces had occupied the country for six years, and his first act was to keep on Bush's defense secretary, Robert Gates, longtime CIA functionary and veteran of the Iran-Contra affair, in the Pentagon. A cruder and more demonstrative signal of political continuity could hardly have been conceived. In the last two years of the Republican administration, US troop levels were increased by 20 percent, to 150,000, in a "surge" that was hailed across the party spectrum as having crushed the Iraqi resistance, readying the country for a stable pro-Western, even democratic, future. The new Democratic administration has not deviated at all from this script. The three-year Status of Forces Agreement signed by Bush and his collaborators in Baghdad had stipulated that all US troops would leave Iraq by December 2011—although a subsequent agreement could obviously extend their stay—and that US "combat" forces would quit Iraqi cities, villages and other localities by June 2009. Before his election, Obama promised a withdrawal of all US "combat" troops from Iraq within sixteen months of his taking office, i.e. by May 2010—adorned with a safety clause that this pledge could be "refined" in the light of events. It promptly was, with the February 2009 announcement that combat forces would now leave Iraq by September 2010, and that the "residual" 50,000 troops could also engage in combat operations to "protect our ongoing civilian and military efforts."[7]

7   Obama speech at Camp Lejeune, North Carolina, February 27, 2009.

The slaughter and devastation wreaked on Iraq by the United States and its allies, chiefly Britain, are now well known: the destruction of the country's cultural patrimony, the brutal dismembering of its social infrastructure, the theft of its natural resources, the sundering of its mixed neighborhoods, and above all the death or displacement of countless of its citizens—over a million dead; three million refugees; five million orphans, according to government figures.[8] Wasting no words on any of this, the commander-in-chief and his generals have other concerns. Can Iraq now be regarded as a tolerably secure outpost of the American system in the Middle East? They have reason to exult, and reason to doubt. Compared with the situation at the height of the insurgency in 2006, most of the country today is under the thumb of Baghdad, and American casualties are few and far between. A predominantly Shia army—some 250,000 strong—has been trained and armed to the teeth to deal with any resurgence of the resistance. Sectarian cleansing of the capital, on a scale of which the Haganah could be proud, has wiped out most Sunni neighborhoods, for the first time giving the Maliki regime set up by Bush a firm grip on the hub of the country. To the north, the Kurdish protectorates remain staunch bastions of US power. To the south, Moqtada al-Sadr's militias have been sent packing. Best of all, the oil wells are returning to those who know how to make good use of them, as auctions distribute twenty-five-year leases to foreign

8   *Cultural Cleansing in Iraq: Why Museums Were Looted, Libraries Burned and Academics Murdered*, edited by Raymond Baker, Shereen Ismael and Tareq Ismael, London, 2009, contains detailed figures and sources, among them the fact that from 2003 to 2007, Washington allowed only 463 refugees, mainly professional Iraqis of Christian origin, into the United States. For an illuminating survey of the history of Iraqi oil and the privatized looting now under way, see Kamil Mahdi, "Iraq's Oil Law: Parsing the Fine Print," *World Policy Journal*, Summer 2007.

corporations. Some excesses may mar the scene in Baghdad,[9] but the new Iraq has the blessing of the saintly Sistani's smile.

Yet there persists the uneasy thought that the Iraqi resistance, capable of inflicting such damage on the US military machine only yesterday, might just be biding its time after its heavy losses and the defection of an important segment, and could still visit havoc on the collaborators tomorrow, should the US pull out altogether.[10] To ensure against any such danger, Washington has put down markers, in the modern equivalents—vastly larger and more hideous—of the Crusader fortresses of old. The Balad military base, within easy bomber reach of Baghdad, is a small-town American city-state. Containing an airport that is reportedly the busiest in the world after Heathrow, it can house over 30,000 US soldiers and auxiliaries—the latter an immigrant labor force composed largely of South Asian workers who clean homes, cook food and staff Subway sandwich bars; drug dealers, too, are never in short supply; mobile Eastern European prostitutes serve Balad's other needs. Fifteen bus routes complement the airport, but commuting

9 These excesses were detailed in an article published in the *Economist* on September 3, 2009, "Could a Police State Return?": "Old habits from Saddam Hussein's era are becoming familiar again. Torture is routine in government detention centres … Iraqi police and security people are again pulling out fingernails and beating detainees, even those who have already made confessions. A limping former prison inmate tells how he realized, after a bout of torture in a government ministry that lasted for five days, that he had been relatively lucky. When he was reunited with fellow prisoners, he saw that many had lost limbs and organs. The domestic-security apparatus is at its busiest since Saddam was overthrown six years ago, especially in the capital. In July the Baghdad police reimposed a nightly curfew, making it easier for the police, taking orders from politicians, to arrest people disliked by the Shia-led government."

10 General Petraeus recently announced that attacks on US forces in Iraq were down to "only" fifteen a day, according to the *Financial Times*, January 2, 2010. Not Maliki but Muntadhar al-Zaidi, the Baghdad shoe-thrower, represents the sentiments of most Iraqis, regardless of ethnic or confessional origin.

remains a problem for some of the service staff.[11] Another thirteen military and air force bases are scattered throughout the country, among them Camp Renegade near Kirkuk, to guard the oil wells; Badraj on the Iranian border, for espionage in the Islamic Republic; and a British base dating back to the 1930s at Nasiriyah, upgraded to serve American appetites. In Baghdad itself, meanwhile, the US proconsul enjoys the largest and most expensive embassy in the world—it is the size of the Vatican City—in the fortified enclave of the Green Zone.

After seizing Iraq as colonial prey in 1920 and installing the Hashemite dynasty as its local instrument, Britain faced a full-scale rebellion, which it suppressed only with difficulty and all-out savagery. For the next twelve years, London ruled the country as an imperial dependency before finally relinquishing its "mandate"—granted by the League of Nations—in 1932. But the client regime it left behind lasted another quarter of a century, until it was finally overthrown in the revolution of 1958. The American seizure of Iraq provoked a full-scale insurgency even more swiftly, and one that has lasted longer, against an occupation enjoying this time the mandate of the United Nations. The US empire, too, will leave behind a puppet regime to hold down the country for the foreseeable future. In that venture, there could be few more fitting successors to Ramsay MacDonald—that earlier handsome, willowy figure who was never at a loss for uplifting words—than Barack Obama. But history has accelerated since those days, and there is at

---

11 "It takes the masseuse, Mila from Kyrgyzstan, an hour to commute to work by bus on this sprawling American base. Her massage parlor is one of three on the base's 6,300 acres and sits next to a Subway sandwich shop in a trailer, surrounded by blast walls, sand and rock." Marc Santora, "Big US Bases Are Part of Iraq, but a World Apart," *New York Times*, September 8, 2009.

least a chance that Maliki and his torturers will meet the fate of Nuri al-Said more rapidly, in another national uprising to root out alien military bases, outsize embassies, oil companies and their local collaborators alike.

This will not happen overnight, but the popularity given the shoe-thrower, for restoring a semblance of national pride, should not be underestimated. The Iraqi elections of 2010 pitted Prime Minister Nouri al-Maliki against Ayad Allawi, a former prime minister and CIA agent who was accused of personally executing political prisoners soon after the occupation of the country. Allawi's bloc—backed by some local Sunni groups and the Saudis—emerged as the largest single group in parliament. According to some sources, the US Embassy was not unhappy with the outcome.

Maliki, a long-term collaborator with the occupiers, was not far behind, but his failure, despite heavy rigging and the use of security forces inside polling booths, was widely viewed in the region as a stinging defeat.[12] After it, he flew to Tehran to seek refuge under the Iranian umbrella. Maneuverings began immediately to construct an alliance of Shia groups that had a comfortable overall majority. Moqtada al-Sadr agreed to this but only if Maliki stepped down as prime minister. Four months after the elections, Iraq was still waiting for a new puppet government with one set of strings worked by Washington and the other by Tehran.

For American elites, Iran has long posed a conundrum: an "Islamic Republic" publicly breathing fire against the Great Satan while quietly extending assistance to it wherever most needed, be

---

12   Oliver August, "Election Monitors' Report Increases Doubts over Fairness of Iraqi Election," TimesOnline.com, March 15, 2010.

it collusion with counterrevolutionaries in Nicaragua, invasion of Afghanistan or occupation of Iraq. The rulers of Israel are not the recipients of any of these benefits, and have taken a dimmer view of the rhetoric of the mullahs, which is directed with greater ferocity at them and at the Little Satan in London than at their patrons in Washington. Above all, once the prospect of an Iranian nuclear program undermining the Israeli monopoly of weapons of mass destruction in the Middle East started to loom on the horizon, Tel Aviv galvanized its assets in the United States into a campaign to ensure that Washington became committed to striking the program down at all costs. Not that there was much resistance to overcome, given the degree to which Israeli objectives have long been internalized as little less than second nature by US policymakers. Scorning overtures from the Khatami regime for an across-the-board regional deal in 2003, the Republican administration sought instead to force Iran into compliance with the Israeli monopoly by answering Tehran's oratorical tirades with tirades of its own and tightening its economic sanctions on Iran.

Without saying so too explicitly, Obama came into office allowing it to be understood that he thought this was not the way to go about things. Much better would be to initiate a forgive-and-forget dialogue with Tehran, banking on the traditional pragmatism of the regime and the manifest pro-Americanism of the middle-class and youth layers in the population at large, in order to achieve a friendly diplomatic settlement in the interest of all parties, denuding Iran of nuclear capability in exchange for an economic and political embrace. But the timing was unlucky and the calculation was upset by political polarization in Iran itself. Factional struggles in the clerical establishment escalated over the presidential election in June 2009, when a bid by its most openly pro-Western wing to take power on a wave of (mostly) middle-class protest was suppressed by an incumbent counterstrike of electoral fraud and militia violence. For Obama, the opportunity for ideological posturing was too great to resist. In a peerless display of sanctimony, he lamented with moist-eyed grief the death of a demonstrator killed in Tehran on the same day his drones wiped out sixty villagers, most of them women and children, in Pakistan. With the Western media in full cry behind the president, the thwarted candidate in the Iranian contest—historically one of the worst butchers of the regime, responsible for mass executions in the 1980s—was converted into another icon of the Free World. Schemes for a grand reconciliation between the two states had to be set aside.

Following this misadventure, the Democratic administration has reverted to the line of its predecessor, attempting to corral Russia and China—European acquiescence can be taken for granted—into an economic blockade of Iran, in the hope of so strangling the country that the Supreme Leader will either be overthrown or obliged to come to terms. Should such pressure fail, an air strike by Israeli or American bombers on Iranian nuclear facilities remains the backup threat. Although unlikely, such a blitz cannot be altogether ruled out, if only because once the West at large—in this case not only Obama but also Sarkozy, Brown and Merkel—has pronounced any Iranian nuclear capability intolerable, leaving little room for a rhetorical retreat if this capability is achieved.[13]

---

13   In Illinois in 2004, I watched Obama interviewed on network television in the run-up to the Senate election he subsequently won. Asked whether he would back Bush if he decided to bomb Iran, the future president did not hesitate for a moment. He put on a warlike look and said that he would.

In the past, fear of Iranian retaliation against shaky American positions in Iraq would probably have been enough to deter such an assault. But Tehran's influence in Baghdad is not what it was. Once confident that Iraq would shortly become a sister Islamic Republic, it can no longer be sure that relations between the two nations will be any better than between the various Sunni states in the region. The Maliki regime used to know which side buttered its bread—Iran could never match the dollars and arms it gets from the US—and Sistani's pretensions to preeminence over assorted divines across the border are of long standing, but its electoral setback has strengthened Tehran's hand. One of the more comical sights after the latest Iraq elections was a senior US Embassy spokesman, speaking to the press in a heavily fortified Green Zone, warning the Iranians not to interfere with Iraqi sovereignty. Whether Moqtada al-Sadr's militias will move into action failing an accord with the government remains to be seen.

Still, to date the Pentagon remains opposed to any adventure that might string its forces out across a war zone stretching from the Litani to the Oxus, if the Revolutionary Guards were to foment operations in Lebanon or western Afghanistan. Nor should Tehran's threat to retaliate with conventional missiles against Israeli cities be discounted. There are also Washington's other allies to be considered. Israel and its lobbyists may be the prime movers in ongoing agitation against Iran, but they are not alone. The Saudi monarchy, a sui generis confessional dictatorship, remains fearful that a Tehran–Baghdad combination might destabilize the Peninsula: Shia constitute a large majority in Bahrain and in the oil-producing region of the Saudi state itself. But the Saudis are also aware that any direct attack on Tehran could pose an even bigger threat to their rule, provoking Shia uprisings that might engulf them. For Riyadh, an alternative route, now under review in Washington, is preferable: inserting Turkey into the regional equation as a Sunni–NATO detachment of the empire, buttressing the effects of Saudi petrodollars offered to Syria to break with Iran. This would serve as a counterthrust against any future Tehran–Baghdad axis and cut off Hezbollah from Damascus, softening it up for another assault by the IDF. But Turkey, smarting from EU rejection and lack of US support during the flotilla crisis with Israel, has been flexing its muscles, refusing to be lined up against Tehran.

Mainstream discussion of the nuclear issue glosses over the realities of the region. Ahmadinejad reaped a harvest of discontent not only from the corrupt and brutal days of Rafsanjani's presidency but also from the time of his spineless successor. Under the reformer Khatami, economic conditions steadily worsened even as oil prices rose, and Iran's naive overtures in foreign policy merely inspired Bush's Axis of Evil rhetoric, much as Gorbachev's similar attempts prompted Reagan's "Evil Empire." Ready to defend the rights of foreign investors but rarely those of independent newspapers or student demonstrators, given to vacuous dialogues with the Pope on spiritual values but incapable of firm protection of civil rights, Khatami maneuvered ineffectually between contradictory pressures until he had exhausted his moral credit. Ahmadinejad's base in the popular classes embeds a greater social sensibility in the new presidency, but there is no guarantee the practical outcomes will be better. The millions of young, working-class, jobless citizens crammed into overcrowded housing, are in desperate need of a coherent policy of national development. But Islamic voluntarism is not a stable alternative to creeping neoliberalism, and the temptation to ratchet up cultural and political repression to compensate for economic frustration is usually irresistible.

In Iran's sprawling, opaque political system, the presidency is surrounded by competing centers of power, nearly all of them headed by figures more conservative than the incumbent. The Supreme Leader Khamenei does not want to be upstaged by a young firebrand. The mullah–*bazaari* nexus behind Rafsanjani has already thwarted Ahmadinejad's efforts to clean up the Oil Ministry, and remains entrenched in the Expediency Council. The pro-Western middle class that identified with Khatami, after licking its wounds, has been looking for a comeback. All are ready to pounce on any misstep or evidence of inexperience, of which there will be not a few. The social backdrop to such disputes remains tense enough in its own right. The skewed development model inherited from the Shah, battered by nearly a decade of war and then subjected to Rafsanjani's inflationary boom and Khatami's privatizations, has produced a vast black market, an unofficial unemployment rate of 25 percent and a looming agricultural crisis. Students are disaffected, labor is rebellious, and the Arab southwest, the Kurdish and Azeri north, and the Baluchi southeast are simmering, and, as we now know, US intelligence agencies are stoking dissent in these areas to further weaken Tehran. There is ample material in this mess for every kind of domestic and imperial intrigue, aimed at toppling the unwelcome victor of a popular contest. Meanwhile, those Iranians (including the country's best-known filmmaker) who once dreamed of "liberation" through US intervention have taken note of the worsening nightmare in Iraq and ditched that particular option.

But for the moment, it is Iran's external role that holds center stage. Here too the directionless clerical state has left a scene of confusion. Since the end of the Iran–Iraq War, its foreign policy has been little more than a ragbag of incoherent opportunism, combining conventional diplomacy of a cautious, typically collaborationist sort with largely costless gestures of solidarity to fellow-Shia abroad, principally Hezbollah in southern Lebanon, with crumbs for the Palestinians. Tehran was tactfully silent during the Gulf War of 1991, with not even a peep of complaint when US troops were stationed in the Holy Places. It instructed its surrogates in the Northern Alliance to pave the way for the American invasion of Afghanistan. It collaborated with the CIA in preparations for the occupation of Iraq, and directed SCIRI (Supreme Council for the Islamic Revolution in Iraq) and its other political assets to prop up US rule in Baghdad. In exchange for these favors to the Great Satan, what has it received? American armies camped on its eastern and western borders, and American threats to obliterate its reactors.

The partially rigged Iranian elections of 2010 and the repression that followed weakened Ahmadinejad's standing in the country, but without seriously affecting the base of his core support in the country's poor and low-income social layers. More importantly, when forced to choose between the incumbent and Rafsanjani's men, the Supreme Leader, Ayatollah Khamenei, opted firmly for Ahmadinejad. Hopes that the mass mobilization in Tehran might topple the government (if not the clerical regime) were not fulfilled. Meanwhile the US/EU/Israel nexus continued to build support for Ahmadinejad by pushing through a sanctions resolution in the Security Council, weakened by the need to get China and Russia on board.

Even by the standards of today's "international community," the Western campaign to oblige Iran to abandon nuclear research, an option to which Iran is entitled under the Non-Proliferation Treaty, is breathtaking. The country is ringed by atomic states—India, Pakistan, China, Russia, Israel—and American nuclear submarines patrol its southern coast. Historically, it has every reason to fear outside threats. Although neutral, it was occupied by both British and Soviet forces during World War II. Its elected government was overthrown by an Anglo-American coup in 1953, and the secular opposition was destroyed. From 1980 to 1988, the Western powers abetted Saddam Hussein's onslaught, in which hundreds of thousands of Iranians died. In the war's final stages, the US destroyed nearly half the Iranian navy in the Gulf, and for good measure shot down a crowded civilian passenger plane.

At present, Iran has managed little more than primitive gropings toward the technology needed for nuclear self-defense. Yet these were presented as a casus belli by Bush, Blair, Chirac and Olmert, whose own states were armed with hundreds—in the case of the United States, thousands—of nuclear weapons. Whining and caviling over the small print of Vienna protocols, however warranted, has been a futile ploy for Iranian diplomacy. The country would do better to choose the right moment and simply withdraw from the Non-Proliferation Treaty. Of all the anachronistic emperors in the world, that treaty is the most brazenly naked. There is not a shred of justification for the oligopoly of the present nuclear powers, which is so hypocritical it does not dare even speak its name—Israel, with 200 nuclear bombs, is never mentioned. There will never be nuclear disarmament until it is broken.

To face up to the enemies ranged against Iran requires a coherence and discipline of which it shows little sign at present. With their own operational habits and doctrines to the fore, the Iranian clerics have played a profoundly divisive role in keeping the Shia parties and Sistani, Tehran's bearded queen on the Iraqi chessboard, pitted against the resistance forces. A de-confessionalized alliance of forces from Tehran to Damascus, via Basra and Baghdad, would both damp down communalist conflict and strengthen Iran's position. Little in the recent Iranian record suggests that the country's ruling institutions are capable of dealing with imperial arrogance when they confront it, other than with a hydra-headed incompetence. However, circumstances may now be forcing them into decisions they have so far sought to evade. It will not be easy to dress up surrender to Western threats as dignified national wisdom. It will not be difficult to turn Shia crowds and militia against the Western occupation across the border. Tehran controls more significant hostages today than a mere embassy. It is unlikely, if the country kept its nerve, that the Pentagon or its proxies would risk an attack.

The pressure for an assault on Iran comes from Israel and its US proxies. The Pentagon, aware of the dangers, has resisted all such calls, and Admiral Mullen was moved sideways for saying as much in public. Russia and China backed the watered-down sanctions in the Security Council to circumvent any possibility of a military attack. Were Obama to cave on Iran and order or approve a bombing raid on Tehran he would be signing his own political death-warrant and acting against what serious and rational conservatives regard as real US interests in the region. The consequences would be dire at home and abroad.

From Palestine through Iraq to Iran, Obama has acted as just another steward of the American empire, pursuing the same aims as his predecessors, with the same means but with a more emollient rhetoric. In Afghanistan, he has gone further, widening the front of imperial aggression with a major escalation of violence, both technological and territorial. When he took office, Afghanistan had already been occupied by US and satellite forces for more than seven years. During his election campaign Obama—determined to outdo Bush in prosecuting a "just war"—pledged more troops and fire power to crush the Afghan resistance, and more ground intrusions and drone attacks in Pakistan to burn out support for it across the border. This is one promise he has kept. A further 30,000 troops are currently being rushed to the Hindu Kush. This will bring the US army of occupation close to 100,000, under a general picked by Obama for the success of his brutalities in Iraq, where his units formed a specialist elite in assassination and torture. Simultaneously, a massive intensification of aerial terror over Pakistan is under way. As the *New York Times* informed its readers, delicately describing the statistic as one "that the White House has not advertised": "since Mr. Obama came to office, the Central Intelligence Agency has mounted more Predator drone strikes into Pakistan than during Mr. Bush's eight years in office."[14] These were justified in March 2009 by Harold Koh, a former dean of Yale Law School and a former director of the Orville H. Schell, Jr. Center for Human Rights, and now a senior lawyer attached to the State Department. The unmanned drone strikes supposedly targeting terrorists were lawful, he argued, because they were necessary to defend US national security. Most of those killed have been civilians, including men, women and children. In January 2010 the house and family of a journalist in Peshawar was

14   David Sanger, "Obama Outlines a Vision of Might and Right," *New York Times*, December 11, 2009.

destroyed by one such attack. Most liberal newspapers and TV networks obediently failed to report the event for fear of encouraging "anti-Americanism," already at a peak in the country. Koh's obscene speech defending the legality of drone attacks was delivered deadpan to the American Society for International Law in March 2010, where it received warm applause.[15]

There is no mystery about the reason for this escalation. After invading Afghanistan in 2001, the US and its European auxiliaries imposed a puppet government of their own making, confected at a conference in Bonn, headed by a CIA asset and seconded by an assortment of Tajik warlords, with NGOs in attendance like page boys in a medieval court. This bogus construct never had the slightest legitimacy in the country, lacking even a modicum of the narrow but dedicated base the Taliban had enjoyed. Once installed in Kabul, it concentrated its energies on self-enrichment. Aid was diverted, corruption generalized, narcotics—suppressed by the Taliban—set free. Karzai and company amassed a huge amount of wealth: over 75 percent of the funds from donor countries were handed directly to Karzai's cronies, the Northern Alliance or private contractors used by both. The construction of a new five-star hotel and a shopping mall became priorities in one of the world's poorest countries, while torture and murder proceeded routinely a short distance away: Bagram has become a

---

15 Chase Madar, "How Liberal Law Professors Kill," *Counterpunch*, May 14–16, 2010. Madar noted: "From his throne at Yale Law, Koh inveighed against the unlawful use of torture, against the unlawful invasion of Iraq, against the unlawful detentions at Guantanamo. (He has argued that the US risks a permanent spot on the 'axis of disobedience' for its chronic flouting of international law.) If it had been W. intensifying the drone strikes in Central Asia, one can easily imagine Koh condemning this practice as yet another brazen violation of that same law."

chamber of horrors that makes Guantánamo look civilized. Opium production reached an all-time high, soaring to over 90 percent above its levels in 2001, when it was still confined to areas controlled by the Northern Alliance, spreading southward and westward under the aegis of the Karzai clan. The mass of the Afghan poor have received little or nothing from the new foreign-imposed order except increased risk to life and limb, as the reorganized Taliban hits back at the occupation and NATO bombs rain so indiscriminately on villages that even Karzai has repeatedly been forced to protest.[16]

By June 2009 the Afghan guerrillas controlled large swathes of the country and had infiltrated official police and military units. Adopting Iraqi tactics of placing IEDs on the roads and suicide bombs in the cities, they were inflicting ever heavier blows on the Western occupation and its collaborators. Matthew Hoh, a former Marine captain who served as a political officer in Iraq and subsequently Afghanistan, and resigned in September 2009, wrote in a letter:

> The Pashtun insurgency, which is composed of multiple, seemingly infinite, local groups, is fed by what is perceived by the Pashtun people as a continued and sustained assault, going back centuries, on Pashtun land, culture, traditions and religion by internal and external enemies … In both the East and South, I have observed that the bulk of the insurgency fights not for the white banner of the Taliban, but rather against the presence of foreign soldiers and taxes imposed by an unrepresentative government in Kabul … If honest, our stated strategy of securing Afghanistan to prevent al-Qaeda resurgence or regrouping

16 Most recently on December 27, 2009, when a US black-ops unit killed ten civilians on the same day that Ahmadinejad's militias killed five demonstrators in Tehran.

would require us to additionally invade and occupy western Pakistan, Somalia, Sudan, Yemen, etc.[17]

Meanwhile, within the imperial camp itself, confusion was mounting. American diplomatic and military functionaries publicly contradicted each other, quarreling over how far the pretence of democratic elections staged by Karzai should be upheld or rejected. In the event, after vehement denunciations of fraud by the highest State Department functionary in Washington, and a pro forma second round of voting, Obama consummated the farce by congratulating Karzai on a victory more blatantly rigged even than Ahmadinejad's two months earlier, on which—in top Pecksniff form—the US president had not stinted stern words. Unlike the regime in Tehran, which retains an indigenous base in society, however diminished, what passes for government in Kabul is a Western implant that would disintegrate overnight without the NATO praetorians dispatched to protect it.

Aware that Washington might decided to cut its losses sooner rather than later—despite the huge lithium deposits recently uncovered by US geologists excavating the country—and do a deal with the insurgents, Karzai and his brother began their own negotiations with the Taliban, after which they suggested that the US remove their leaders, including Mullah Omar, from the Most Wanted list and allow them to travel freely as ordinary citizens of the country. General Eikenberry, the proconsul in Kabul, did not rule this out but insisted it was only possible on an individual basis. That things have gone this far is in itself an indication of the precariousness of the situation. Another straw in the wind was the increasing number of hints from the ever-loyal British that things

17 Ralph Nader, "Hoh's Afghanistan Warning," *CounterPunch*, November 4, 2009.

could not go on as they were. A senior British intelligence chief publicly ridiculed the British government position elaborated by former Prime Minister Gordon Brown: that British troops were in Afghanistan to prevent terrorist attacks on Britain. Most serious observers know full well that it was Blair's and Brown's involvement in two murderous wars that made the country vulnerable to attacks from within. Throughout Europe, including countries like Poland, a large majority of citizens are opposed to the presence of their troops in Afghanistan. The CIA's confidential PR memorandum for winning over European public opinion is kindergarten stuff that has already been tried and raises even more questions regarding the occupation and its failures:

> Afghan women could serve as ideal messengers in humanizing the ISAF role in combating the Taliban because of women's ability to speak personally and credibly about their experiences under the Taliban, their aspirations for the future, and their fears of a Taliban victory. Outreach initiatives that create media opportunities for Afghan women to share their stories with French, German, and other European women could help to overcome pervasive skepticism among women in Western Europe toward the ISAF mission.
>
> According to INR polling in the fall of 2009, French women are 8 percentage points less likely to support the mission than are men, and German women are 22 percentage points less likely to support the war than are men.
>
> Media events that feature testimonials by Afghan women would probably be most effective if broadcast on programs that have large and disproportionately female audiences.[18]

---

18 "CIA Red Cell: A Red Cell Special Memorandum/Confidential/No Foreign Nationals" was released by WikiLeaks on March 26, 2010.

Desperate to claim victory in a self-chosen "just war," Obama has plunged into the classic *fuite en avant* of dispatching a still larger expeditionary force and expanding the war to a neighboring country where the enemy was suspected of finding succor. From the start of his administration, he announced that Pakistan and Afghanistan would henceforward be treated as an integrated war zone, "Afpak." A stream of emissaries poured into Islamabad to man up the Pakistani state to the repressive tasks it was being called upon to perform.[19]

What Obama failed to grasp was that there were sound reasons to explain Bush's inability to defeat the Afghan insurgency. This had little to do with his Iraq "obsession." It was the result of a history and geography willfully ignored by imperial strategists.

The 1,528-mile border between Afghanistan and what is now Pakistan has been porous ever since the Durand Line was laid down by the British Empire in 1893. Sixteen million Pashtuns live in southern Afghanistan, 28 million in the Northwest Frontier Province of Pakistan. The frontier is impossible to police, and movement across it difficult to detect, since tribes that speak the same dialect and are often intermarried live on either side. That Afghan insurgents seek and receive sanctuary in the area is hardly a secret. For NATO or the Pakistani Army to stop this flow would require at least a quarter of a million troops, and campaigns of annihilation like those of Chiang Kai-shek in the 1930s. Under Musharraf—

19 Mercenary outfits were dispatched to speed up the process. Inter-Risk, the Pakistani subsidiary of US defense contractor DynCorp, was recently raided by local police, who seized "illegal and sophisticated weaponry." The company's boss, a retired Captain Ali Jaffar Zaidi, informed reporters that US officials in Islamabad had ordered the import of prohibited weapons "in Inter-Risk's name" promising that payment would be made by the US embassy. See Anwar Abbasi, "Why the US Security Company Was Raided," *The News*, September 20, 2009.

and threats from Pentagon blowhards to bomb the country back into the Stone Age if it did not comply—the Pakistani Army was turned from patron to foe of the Taliban in Afghanistan, but never a wholehearted foe, since it was only too well aware that it was being forced to yield its influence on Kabul to India, which wasted no time in taking Karzai under its wing. Musharraf did his best to please America by allowing US Special Forces and drones into the country and handing over al-Qaeda operatives where he could. But he never really satisfied Washington that he was being vigilant enough, and meanwhile managed to earn the contempt of the majority of Pakistanis for truckling to the US.

By the time Obama came to power, two developments had altered this scene. Incessantly goaded by the Pentagon, between 2004 and 2006 Musharraf sent the Pakistani Army nine times into the Federally Administered Tribal Areas (FATA), the seven mountainous sectors outside the jurisdiction of the Northwest Frontier Province, where central governmental authority had always been vestigial, to crack down on Taliban infiltration, which simply provoked in the region's inhabitants a sense of solidarity with the Afghan resistance and an increasing will to emulate it. In December 2007 they formed the Tehrik-i-Taliban Pakistan (TTP), a brutal homegrown guerrilla force dedicated to carrying the war back against Islamabad itself. (Contrary to Western assumptions, this outfit is not a subsidiary of the Afghan neo-Taliban, as evidenced by Mullah Omar's outburst against it. Revealingly, Omar insisted that it was wrong to target the Pakistani Army when the real enemy was the US and NATO.)

In 2008, Musharraf himself was ousted, fleeing to Mecca to avoid impeachment and later moving to London, where after a short time the British withdrew his security detail. He was replaced as president by the infamous widower of Benazir Bhutto, Asif Zardari, a discredited crook who offered himself as an ideal straw man for the US. Washington's ambassador, Anne Patterson (fresh from her duty arming Uribe in Colombia), was soon gushing over his cooperative goodwill. Its fruits were not long in coming. In April 2009, Zardari ordered the Army to occupy the Swat district in the Northwest Frontier Province, taken over by the TTP two months earlier. An all-out military assault drove the TTP back into the hills and two million refugees out of their homes. Emboldened by this humanitarian success, Obama pressured Zardari into sending the Army into FATA proper, in October, to flush out Taliban fighters—it no longer mattered much whether Afghan or Pakistani—from South Waziristan and Bajaur. Hundreds of thousands more tribespeople were displaced, US bombers roaring overhead as they scattered to the winds.[20] In November the Pakistan Army announced, "The offensive is over." The guerrillas had disappeared.

How far domestic ethnic cleansing of this sort can be taken, and what kind of results it is likely to produce, has yet to be seen. What is clear is that in forcing the Pakistani Army to turn its guns on its own tribes, with whom it used to be on fairly good terms, Obama is destabilizing yet another society in the interests of the American empire. Suicide bombs are now exploding on a weekly basis in Pakistan's big cities, in vain acts of revenge for repression on the frontier. Zardari and his entourage are tottering, as the immunity against corruption charges granted them by Musharraf has been

20 For the estimated number of refugees in Swat and FATA, see Mark Schneider, "FATA 101: When the Shooting Stops," *Foreign Policy*, November 4, 2009. Schneider is senior vice president of the establishment organization International Crisis Group.

struck down by the Pakistan Supreme Court, but is kept going by US support.[21] Were that to be withdrawn too, he would fall within days, but—as in the case of Karzai further north—Washington is reluctant to let such a helpful stooge go. However, if Zardari were to tumble on his own, the US government can no doubt rely on the army's top brass to provide a functional substitute, as it always has in the past, The Pakistani Army has never produced patriotic junior officers of the kind that Latin America or the Arab world has sometimes seen, capable of eliminating the high command, expelling foreign agencies and instituting reforms. Its subservience to the United States is structural, without ever having been total. Dependent on massive infusions of American cash and equipment, it cannot afford to defy Washington openly, even when obliged to act against its own interests; covertly, it always seeks to retain a margin of autonomy, so long as confrontation with India persists. It will harry its own citizens at the behest of the US, but not to the point of setting the tribal areas irretrievably on fire or helping to extirpate all resistance across the border.

So, after the recent expansion, what are the prospects for Obama's "just war"? Comparing the American with the Soviet occupation of Afghanistan, two major differences stand out. The regime created by the US is far weaker than that protected by the USSR. The latter had a genuine local basis, however much it

21 The US-brokered deal that allowed Zardari and his late wife to return to the country during the Musharraf period was pushed through via a hurriedly concocted "National Reconciliation Ordinance" pardoning politicians charged with various crimes. Last November, the National Assembly in Pakistan refused to vote in favor of renewing the ordinance. The reinstated chief justice did the rest. On December 16, 2009, a cold, crisp winter afternoon in Islamabad, the full bench of the Supreme Court of Pakistan—sixteen senior judges and the chief justice—declared the ordinance null and void. Few doubt that the Zardari interregnum is almost over. This particular US drone can now be returned safely to base in Dubai or Manhattan.

abused it: never just an alien graft, the PDPA (People's Demo-cratic Party of Afghanistan) generated an army and administration capable of surviving the departure of Soviet troops. The Najibullah government was eventually overthrown only thanks to massive outside assistance from the US, Saudi Arabia and Pakistan. But in that assistance lies the second decisive contrast. Unlike the fighters who entered Kabul in 1992, bankrolled and armed to the teeth by foreign powers, the Afghan resistance of today is all but completely isolated: anathema not only to Washington but also to Moscow, Beijing, Dushanbe, Tashkent, Tehran—able at most to count on a sporadic, furtive tolerance from Islamabad.

General Stanley McChrystal's kamikaze interview, published by Rolling Stone in June 2010, in which he voiced some indis-creet criticisms of the political leaders at home, had the desired effect. He was recalled and removed as commander in Afghanistan and replaced by his boss, General David Petraeus. But behind this short-lived drama in Washington was a war that had gone badly wrong, and no amount of sweet talk can now hide this fact. The military's loathing for Richard Holbrooke (a Clinton creature) goes deep not because of his personal defects, of which there are many, but because his attempt to dump Karzai without having a serious replacement angered the uniforms. Aware that this war is unwinnable, they were not prepared to see Karzai fall: without a Pashtun point man in the country the collapse might reach Saigon proportions. All the generals know that the stalemate will not be easy to break, but desirous of building reputations and careers and eager to experiment with new weapons and new strategies (real war games are always appealing to the military, provided the risks are small), they have obeyed orders, despite disagreements with each other and the politicians.

Obama's surge was supported by McChrystal and Petraeus, but not by General Eikenberry, the ex-boss of both men and currently ambassador in Kabul. His view has been vindicated by the stalemate and the price being paid in terms of lives. All the media-hyped advances are illusory. US and NATO casualties rise each week; most Europeans and many North American citizens are opposed to the war and favor withdrawal; different factions of the Taliban are preparing to take power; Iran has been alienated by the sanctions and will not play ball anymore; the Northern Alliance is a busted flush, its leaders busy, like the Karzai brothers, making money. And lithium reserves notwithstanding, it is becoming more and more difficult to sustain a NATO presence in the country. Pakistan's military is in permanent talks with the Taliban leadership, and a desperate Karzai has asked the US to remove Mullah Omar and the old Taliban leaders from the list of "terrorists" so they can travel freely and participate in the life of the country. Eikenberry's response: We are prepared to consider each request on its merits, but no blanket amnesty. That, too, will come.[22]

This is why comparisons with Vietnam, though they are telling in so many other respects—moral, political, ideological—in military terms are less so. On one level, Obama's arrogant escalation of the war in Afghanistan could be said to combine the hubris of Kennedy in 1961 with that of Johnson in 1965, even of Nixon in

---

22   In the US, as the midterm elections loomed ahead, Netanyahu's visit was eagerly awaited, expected to help shore up AIPAC support for the beleaguered Democrats. The talk in Washington was that losses at home and abroad might lead Obama to get rid of Gates at the Pentagon and Emanuel at the White House. Would their replacements be any better?

1970, whose bombing of Cambodia shows more than one point of resemblance to current operations in Pakistan. But there is no draft to disaffect mainstream American youth; no Soviet or Chinese aid to sustain the guerrilla; no anti-imperialist solidarity to weaken the system in its homelands. On the contrary, as Obama likes to explain, no fewer than forty-two countries are lending a hand to help his embarrassing marionette in Kabul dance a good show.[23]

No world-historical spectacle could be more welcome than the American proconsul fleeing once again by helicopter from the roof of the embassy, and the motley expeditionary forces and their assorted civilian lackeys kicked unceremoniously out of the country along with him. But a second Saigon is not in prospect. Monotonous talk of the end of American hegemony, the universal cliché of the period, is mostly a way of avoiding mounting a serious opposition to it.

If a textbook illustration were needed of the continuity of American foreign policy across administrations, and the futility of so many softheaded attempts to treat the Bush–Cheney years as exceptional rather than essentially conventional, Obama's conduct has provided it. From one end of the Middle East to the other, the only significant material change he has brought is a further escalation of the War on Terror—or Evil, as he prefers to call it—with Yemen now being sighted as the next target. A new terrorist threat has been discovered there, and strong hints have issued from some

23 In Oslo, Obama could duly congratulate the Nobel Peace Prize committee on the Norwegian troop contingent in Afghanistan, along with those from Albania, Armenia, Australia, Austria, Azerbaijan, Belgium, Bosnia and Herzegovina, Bulgaria, Canada, Croatia, the Czech Republic, Denmark, Estonia, Finland, France, Georgia, Germany, Greece, Hungary, Iceland, Ireland, Italy, Jordan, Latvia, Lithuania, Luxembourg, Macedonia, the Netherlands, New Zealand, Poland, Portugal, Romania, Singapore, Slovakia, Slovenia, Spain, Sweden, Turkey, Ukraine, the United Arab Emirates and the UK.

quarters that an intervention might become necessary. On January 2, 2010, Obama announced the doubling of US military expenditure on Yemen. On December 30, the *Economist* noted, "On his watch American drones and special forces have been busier than ever, not only in Afghanistan and Pakistan but also, it is reported, in Somalia and Yemen."[24]

Beyond, the story is much the same. Renditions—torture by proxy—are upheld as a practice, while the perpetrators of such crimes continue to lounge at their ease in Florida or elsewhere, ignoring extradition warrants under Obama's protection. Domestic wiretaps continue. A coup in Central America is underwritten. New military bases are set up in Colombia. Hillary Clinton jets off to the South and attempts to divide the new Bolivarian states, offering a few crumbs if Ecuador detaches itself from Venezuela.

In the Far East, Japan is still treated as a client state and punished if it seeks to step out of line. Japanese democracy is of no consequence to the imperial bosses in Washington. In February 2010, for instance, the Okinawan parliament (the Prefectural Assembly, elected in 2008) unanimously voted for a special resolution demanding that the US base in Futenma be dismantled and moved elsewhere. A month later, every single mayor in Okinawa's forty-one small towns backed the resolution. In April 2010, the Association of City Mayors, made up of the mayors of the eleven Okinawan cities, reiterated the demand. All to no avail. Okinawa and Japan proper offer a laboratory example of how US hegemony is imposed on a client state.

---

24 *Economist*, "From Shoes to Soft Drinks to Underpants." Slightly alarmed by all this, in February 2010, I went to the Yemen to investigate whether there was a real threat. My report, published in the *London Review of Books*, March 25, 2010, is included in this book as Appendix 2.

Japanese hostility to the US military base in Okinawa was an important factor in the defeat of the Liberal Democratic Party regime in Tokyo last year by the Democratic Party, whose leader, Yukio Hatoyama, had pledged during the campaign to shift the base. He won. Nothing doing, said Defense Secretary Gates, and told Hatoyama's government that the request was "counterproductive" and it was "time to move on." The *Washington Post* dutifully backed this up with a dispatch on April 14, 2010, describing the Japanese leader as "hapless" and "increasingly loopy." During the Brezhnev Era in the former Soviet Union, dissidents were often declared insane and locked up in psychiatric hospitals. The United States simply describes leaders who disagree with it as crazy (Chavez of Venezuela is another example) and tries to topple them. On a visit to Japan, Obama was in imperial mode. He made a public display of understanding Japan's concerns, but in private was much sharper with Hatoyama, who was forced to retract his promise. "Can you follow through?" mocked Obama. Hatoyama said he could, but his ratings plummeted and he resigned after only a few months in office. Another slightly awkward customer had been safely dispatched. This was the first time that the US grip on Okinawa had been challenged since the US–Japan Security Treaty of 1960 that had been forced through parliament under the cover of predawn darkness and in the absence of the opposition parties. For weeks prior to this, Japanese students and trade unionists had snake-danced on the streets of Tokyo protesting against the permanent violation of Japanese sovereignty that was being proposed.[25]

25 "The then US ambassador, Douglas MacArthur II, reported to Washington on Japan as a country whose 'latent neutralism is fed on antimilitarist sentiments, pacifism, fuzzy-mindedness, nuclear neuroses and Marxist bent of intellectuals and educators.'

Obama shows no signs of easing the occupation of Japan, which is still forced to pay the costs of the US base, which total millions of dollars each year. The nuking of Hiroshima and Nagasaki was clearly not enough. The assault on and rape of women in Okinawa will continue.

Still, it would be a mistake to think that nothing has changed. No administration is exactly like any other, and each president leaves a stamp on his own. Substantively, vanishingly little of American imperial dominion has altered under Obama.[26] But propagandistically, there has been a significant upgrade. It is no accident that a leading columnist—and one of the more intelligent—could, only half ironically, list the five most important events of 2009 as so many speeches by Obama.[27] In Cairo, at West Point, in Oslo, the world has been treated to one uplifting homily after another, each address larded with every egregious euphemism that White House speechwriters could muster to describe

The memory of that 1960 crisis has deterred both governments from submitting the relationship to parliamentary or public review ever since." Available online at www.japanfocus.org. Gavan McCormack's long essay "Ampo at 50: The Faltering US-Japan Relationship" is the most detailed account to date.

26 Hence in part the disenchantment of many erstwhile Obama partisans, which has surfaced with striking rapidity compared with the relatively long liberal love affair with Bill Clinton. Nonetheless, in their explanations they have tended to blame structural constraints rather than the incumbent himself: Garry Wills sees the well-meaning president as caught in the cogs of the US imperial state apparatus ("The Entangled Giant," *New York Review of Books*, October 8, 2009), and Frank Rich has angrily attacked lobbyists for undermining Obama's "promise to make Americans trust the government again" ("The Rabbit Ragu Democrats," *New York Times*, October 3, 2009). For Tom Hayden, the "expedient" decision to boost force levels in Afghanistan is "the last in a string of disappointments" (despite the fact that Obama had pledged to do so in his campaign), but though Hayden is removing his bumper sticker, he will still be "supporting Obama down the road" ("Obama's Afghanistan Escalation," *Nation*, December 1, 2009).

27 Gideon Rachman, "The Grim Theme Linking the Year's Main Events," *Financial Times*, December 23, 2009.

America's glowing mission in the world and make a modest avowal of awe and the sense of responsibility in carrying it forward.

"We must say openly to each other the things we hold in our hearts" is the characteristic tone. "Our country has borne a special burden in global affairs. We have spilled American blood in many countries on multiple continents. We have spent our revenue to help others rebuild from rubble and develop their own economies. We have joined with others to develop an architecture of institutions—from the United Nations to NATO to the World Bank—that provide for the common security and prosperity of human beings." "The struggle against violent extremism will not be finished quickly, and it extends well beyond Afghanistan and Pakistan ... Our effort will involve disorderly regions, failed states, diffuse enemies." "Our cause is just, our resolve unwavering. We will go forward with the confidence that right makes might." In the Middle East, there are "tensions" (the term recurs nine times in his address to Mubarak's claque at al-Azhar), and there is a "humanitarian crisis" in Gaza. But "the Palestinians must renounce violence" and "the Iraqi people are ultimately better off" for American actions. In Oslo: "Make no mistake: evil does exist in the world"; "To say that force may sometimes be necessary is not a call to cynicism—it is a recognition of history, the imperfections of man and the limits of reason."[28] In Cairo: "Resistance

28 The tropes of "imperfect man" and "limited reason" are borrowed from the vaporings of Reinhold Niebuhr, pastor of Cold War consciences (see Gopal Balakrishnan, "Sermons on the Present Age," *New Left Review*, January/February 2010). Niebuhr could, however, on occasion be less of a humbug than his pupil. Rather than pious guff about the "two suffering peoples," he had the honesty to call a Zionist spade a spade: in an article in the *Nation* (February 28, 1942), he wrote that "the Anglo-Saxon hegemony that is bound to exist in the event of an Axis defeat will be in a position to see to it that Palestine is set aside for the Jews," adding that "Zionist

72

through violence and killing is wrong." In short: if the US and Israel wage war or bump off leaders they dislike, it is a regrettable moral duty. If Palestinians, Iraqis or Afghans resist them, it is an immoral dead end. As Obama likes to say, "We are all God's children," and "This is God's vision."[29]

If sonorous banality and armor-plated hypocrisy are the hallmarks of this president's style, that does not make the style less functional for the task of servicing and repairing the imperial institutions over which Obama and Hillary Clinton now preside. Nothing grated more on international opinion than the lack of requisite unction with which Bush and Cheney all too often went about their business, exposing allies and audiences otherwise well disposed toward American leadership to inconvenient truths they would have preferred not to hear. Historically, the model for the current variant of imperial presidency is Woodrow Wilson, no less pious a Christian, whose every second word was peace, democracy or self-determination, while his armies invaded Mexico, occupied Haiti and attacked Russia, and his treaties handed one colony after another to his partners in war. Obama is a hand-me-down version of the same, without even Fourteen Points to betray. But cant still goes a long way to satisfy those who yearn for it, as the award to Obama of what García Márquez once called the Nobel Prize for War has graphically shown. After lying enough to voters—promising peace and delivering war—Wilson was

---

leaders are unrealistic in insisting that their demands entail no 'injustice' to the Arab population." The latter would have to be "otherwise compensated."

29 Citations drawn from: "Remarks by the President on a New Beginning," Cairo, June 4, 2009; "Remarks by the President to the Nation on the Way Forward in Afghanistan and Pakistan," West Point, December 1, 2009; Nobel Peace Prize acceptance speech, Oslo, December 11, 2009; "Remarks by the President to the Ghanaian Parliament," Accra, June 11, 2009.

reelected to a second term, though it did not end well for him. In more combative times, Johnson was forced to step down in ignominy for his warmongering, without being able to gull the electors again. Twelve years later, a debacle in Tehran helped sink Carter. If the recent setbacks for Democrats in West Virginia and New Jersey—where Democratic voters stayed at home—become a pattern, Obama could be a third one-term president, abandoned by his supporters and mocked by those he has tried so hard to conciliate.

3

SURRENDER AT HOME:
A ONE-DIMENSIONAL POLITICIAN

In Aeschylus' *Prometheus Bound*, the pathetic figure of Hermes, the messenger-servant of the gods, appeals to the dissident Prometheus to make his peace with the supreme beings of the time. The response from the chained figure, punished for betraying the secret of fire to humans, is exemplary: "Be sure of this, I would not change my evil plight for your servility. It is better to be slave to the rock than to serve Father Zeus as his faithful messenger."

A modern American president—Republican or Democrat— operates as the messenger-servant of the country's corporations, defending them against their critics and ensuring that no obstacles are placed in their way. Since the right to profit is considered sacrosanct, any serious alternative is automatically rejected. This is the permanent tension that lies at the heart of a capitalist democracy and is exacerbated in times of crisis. In order to ensure the survival of the richest, it is democracy that has to be heavily regulated rather than capitalism. The inhuman exigencies of the system preclude policies that would obviously benefit a majority of the population. There have been exceptional conjunctures in the past, where a combination of domestic crisis and radical demands from below push an administration in a reformist direction, but their frequency is limited. The New Deal measures in the 1930s and the Civil Rights Act three decades later were the results of action from below.

Unable and unwilling to deliver any serious reforms, Obama has become the master of the sympathetic gesture, the understanding smile, the pained but friendly expression that always appeared to say, "Really, I agree and wish we could, but we can't. We really can't and it's not my fault." The implication is always that the Washington system prevents any change that he could believe in. But the ring of truth is absent. Whether seriously considering escalating an unwinnable war, bailing out Wall Street, getting the insurance company lobbyists to write the new "health care" bill or suggest nominations to his cabinet and the Supreme Court, the mechanism he has deployed is always the same. A better option is put on the table for show, but not taken seriously. A worse option is rapidly binned. And a supposed compromise emerges. This creates the impression among party loyalists that the prez is doing his best, that a team of serious thinkers is hard at work considering every possibility, but that the better alternative simply isn't feasible. This is followed by the spin doctors coming down hard to defend some shoddy compromise or other.

Perhaps all this is meant to demonstrate what he meant when he wrote in his campaign-oriented book *The Audacity of Hope* that Reagan was a model in many ways. He alone had truly understood the American psyche and for that reason was worthy of admiration. This Clinton-style demagoguery was designed largely to appeal to Republican or swing voters. Thinking of his reelection even before he'd entered the White House, he was determined to be a "consensual" president, unlike Reagan, or for that matter

Lincoln. The latter had led a brutal civil war to preserve the Union, the former had—with the aid of a ruthless conservative politburo—begun to dismantle the New Deal consensus and talked of destroying the Evil Empire.

Thus an inbuilt pragmatism and brazen opportunism were already much in evidence during Obama's days as an Illinois state senator. Rickie Hendon, an African American fellow senator, described his anger on watching four Democrats vote in favor of draconian Republican cuts on child-welfare spending. All four were considered to be "progressive." The only nonwhite was Obama:

> He was running for the United States Senate at the time, and when I asked him with my sad eyes and perplexed, torn heart, he told me he did it because, "We have to be fiscally prudent." I said, "Huh?" and he explained to me that we had to show fiscal responsibility during tough budget times … Finally, I heard the bill number for a cut in the South Side in Senator Obama's district. Barack rose to his feet, and towering over the senate, gave a heart-wrenching speech condemning this particular cut … he asked for compassion and understanding … his fiscally prudent vote took place only about ten minutes earlier and now he wants compassion!

Obama lost the vote, and sharp words were exchanged with Hendon:

> Barack leaned over and stuck his jagged, strained face into my space and told me in an eerie, dark voice that came from some secret place within the ugly side of him, "You embarrassed me on the Senate floor and if you ever do it again I will kick your ass!" I said, "What?" He said, "You heard me, [expletive], and if you come back here by the telephones, where the press can't see it, I'll kick your ass right now!"

Hendon (who is five-foot-seven) agreed to the duel. The two state senators squared up for an impromptu boxing match. Fisticuffs ensued and continued till another senator rushed over and dragged them apart. Obama then suggested that they continue the fight elsewhere so that he could "stomp me into oblivion." The history of Chicago is replete with citizens being stomped into oblivion: literally in the days of Prohibition-era gangsters and politically by the deadly Daley machine. Hendon understood that different destinies awaited him and his colleague: "Barack and I never talked about it again, but in this incident, he proved himself to be bipartisan enough and white enough to be president of the United States to me."[1]

What the episode reveals is that Obama's aggression is reserved for progressives on his own side, a right uppercut waiting to be deployed against those on his left. As for the rest, it's business as usual. Corporations of every sort and the politicians and lobbyists attached to them will never be stomped into oblivion. Instead they're raised on stilts. To the continuities in foreign policy we can add their equivalents on the domestic front. Simultaneously wily and timorous, Obama has succeeded in doing the opposite of what he intended. He wanted to please Democrats and Republicans alike; instead he ended up annoying most of them. The Right has been openly contemptuous, the Center, represented by senior columnists in the *New York Times*, has become surprisingly critical early on (though always in an understanding way), and his own youthful base are becoming alienated. Rhetoric is not enough.

1   Rickey Hendon, *Black Enough/White Enough: The Obama Dilemma*, Chicago, 2009.

The situation at home demands more. All he has been able to offer are Clinton-style policies already discredited.

Identity politics alone is never a sufficient gauge to determine the health of a nation-state. The fact that the United States is less racist, less homophobic and less sexist than it was a hundred years ago is a cause for some celebration, but all this is dramatically counterbalanced by the growing disparity in wealth, which has created a poverty that is brutally punished, as evidenced in the incarceration rate of African Americans in proportion to their presence in the population as a whole:

> In certain crucial ways the United States is more unequal than it was 40 years ago. No group dedicated to ending economic inequality would be thinking today about declaring victory and going home. In 1969, the top quintile of American wage-earners made 43 percent of all the money earned in the US; the bottom quintile made 4.1 percent. In 2007, the top quintile made 49.7 percent; the bottom quintile made 3.4 percent. And while this inequality is both raced and gendered, it's less so than you might think. White people, for example, make up about 70 percent of the US population, and 62 percent of those in the bottom quintile. Progress in fighting racism hasn't done them any good; it hasn't even been designed to do them any good. More generally, even if we succeeded completely in eliminating the effects of racism and sexism, we would not thereby have made any progress towards economic equality. A society in which white people were proportionately represented in the bottom quintile (and black people proportionately represented in the top quintile) would not be more equal; it would be exactly as unequal. It would not be more just; it would be proportionately unjust.[2]

2 Walter Benn Michaels, "What Matters," *London Review of Books*, August 27, 2009.

Consensus politicians never challenged this reality; meanwhile, basically conservative African American groups like Farrakhan's Nation of Islam stressed that the real problem lay within each African American man and as such was best solved individually: this was the message preached at the end of the Million Man March in October 1995. Years later the statistics suggest that the impact of this march was nil. Given the weak and pathetic ideology that rooted it, failure was inevitable. It garnered a great deal of support from establishment pundits and politicians, some of whom openly exulted that the blacks were accepting some responsibility for their condition. A more nuanced version of the same outlook informed Obama as well, and he made a few bad speeches along these lines, but newer and more serious problems were already visible on the horizon. Dark clouds had appeared, presaging an economic thunderstorm.

Even as Obama was busy courting the electorate, Wall Street and the system it had created in the last decades of the twentieth century were in dire trouble. A number of serious economists had been warning for some time that the debt-generated bubble masked a catastrophic decline in investment and profits and was likely to burst sooner rather than later. That the system was pregnant with disaster became clear in the nine months following June 2007, when the waters burst. The large investment banks and up-market brokerages hemorrhaged badly, rapidly losing $175 billion of capital. Half-baked rescue operations by the Federal Reserve stemmed the flow of blood, but not for long.

In September 2008, as the presidential campaign approached its peak, Lehman Brothers imploded. A lame-duck Bush administration decided to let them go under. Had the firm's arrogant and overconfident CEO, Richard Fuld, seriously contemplated a jump from the top floor in the manner of some capitalist barons in 1929? A few months after the collapse, some of his colleagues would, after a few cocktails, recount how, as they tiptoed into his top-floor office, they had seen Fuld staring blankly out of the window as if he might jump. This was retro wishful thinking. This was not 1929. Those suicidal capitalists had more of a conscience than their latter-day successors. They found it difficult to face a future where they might be queuing to beg for a spare dime or join their workers, whose lives they had wrecked, on the scrap heap. Why should Fuld jump, regardless of the handful of demonstrators outside urging him to do so, when his personal treasury, in polar contrast to the US economy, was in overflow mode? Nor were the economists and brokers on the Lehman payroll short of a buck or two. As the Lehman collapse triggered a global panic, Federal Reserve figures revealed that total debt had risen from 255.3 percent of GDP in 1997 to 352.6 percent in 2007. A deregulated financial sector, dizzy with success, had been responsible for fueling the most rapid debt growth that the economy had ever experienced.

An International Monetary Fund honcho warned that the entire capitalist world was "on the brink of a systemic meltdown." In the United States, the Bush administration authorized a government rescue of the mortgage giants Fannie Mae and Freddie Mac, after their shares nosedived. Citigroup was similarly rescued, and rapid shotgun weddings—Merrill Lynch with the Bank of America, HBOS with Lloyds TSB—were performed. Huge infusions of Treasury funds were required to save Goldman Sachs, Deutsche Bank and the Société General. As world output, trade, investment and credit became paralyzed, unemployment figures in the North leaped skyward. The market had failed miserably. State intervention in the shape of trillions of dollars was now required to bandage the system. The much vaunted Washington Consensus was surely dead. Was it? If ever there was an opportunity to embark on a new course, here it was staring the world in the face, a world that desperately needed to be remade. It was political leadership that was lacking. Even Joseph Stiglitz's soft Keynesian approach was regarded as too radical and ignored. He had argued that

> several steps can be taken to reduce foreclosures. First, housing can be made more affordable for poor and middle-income Americans by converting the mortgage deduction into a cashable tax credit. The government effectively pays 50 percent of the mortgage interest and real estate taxes for upper-income Americans, yet does nothing for the poor. Second, bankruptcy reform is needed to allow homeowners to write down the value of their homes and stay in their houses. Third, government could assume part of a mortgage, taking advantage of its lower borrowing costs ...
>
> The new view is that real value can be created by un-slicing and un-dicing—pulling these assets out of the financial system and turning them over to the government. But that requires overpaying for the assets, benefiting only the banks ... Wall Street has polluted the economy with toxic mortgages. It should pay for the cleanup.
>
> There is a growing consensus among economists that any bailout based on Paulson's plan won't work. If so, the huge increase in the national debt and the realization that even $700 billion is not enough to rescue the US economy will erode confidence further and aggravate its weakness. But it is impossible for politicians to do nothing in such a crisis. So we may have to pray that an agreement crafted with the toxic mix of special interests, misguided economics, and right-wing ideologies that produced the crisis can somehow produce a rescue plan that works—or whose failure doesn't do too much damage.[3]

3   Joseph Stiglitz, "Bail-Out Blues," *Guardian*, September 30, 2008.

The visionless politicians of the "center-left" in North America and Europe had expended their entire political capital defending the neoliberal system: Clinton, Blair and Brown, Jospin and Strauss-Kahn, D'Alema and Prodi, Felipe Gonzales and others had all led from the front, dismantling controls and embarking on an orgy of get-rich-quick measures while in office or promising to do so as soon as it was possible. Their heirs were paralyzed. Bush, Brown and Berlusconi had no opposition worth the name. They carried on just as before. Obama's rhetoric was impressive, but no alternative plan was mapped for the electorate. He promised little but insisted that only the Democrats could pull the economy out of the recession, and he made sure the TV cameras caught him as often as possible engaged in deep conversation with Warren Buffett and Paul Volcker, the two figures whose reputations had survived the crisis. More importantly, Obama and his team of advisers (he deliberately excluded Joseph Stiglitz, to avoid sending the wrong message to Wall Street, one presumes) were incapable of developing any serious economic alternative. It was not that the economic mess had not been foreseen.

Over a quarter of a century ago, the late Hyman P. Minsky, a distinguished scholar at the Levy Institute at Bard College till his death in 1996, had developed his "financial-instability hypothesis," warning against the much celebrated financial deregulation and comparing the avatars of financial capital to arsonists busy lighting a fire underneath the economy. Wall Street's casino-style practices were encouraging too much risk-taking. Minsky's argument was clear and prescient: during a long period of prosperity, investors become foolhardy, their portfolios overcrowded with risk, and the amounts they lend are much larger than the borrowers' income can handle. When over-indebted investors are forced to sell stocks to make good on their loans, markets begin spiraling downward, creating a severe demand for cash; this point in the cycle became known as a Minsky moment. Neoliberals denounced him as a nutty radical, living in the past. Recent experience teaches the opposite. Minsky had argued in favor of serious regulation to keep the banks under control, accompanied by a public utility–centered capitalism.

If ever there was a moment for a set of measures enacted on the basis of Minsky's analysis, this was surely it, but US politics had for many decades been based on the needs of corporate capitalism, with the government as a supportive, rather than a controlling, force. The economy was wedded to militarism and financial-ization. The political and personal culture of this period had seen the market openly entering every space including the bedroom (via the new slim-line communication technology). In brief, there was no serious opposition in the country.

Obama was on safe ground when he backed the $700 billion Bush bailout. Among some Democrats there was much talk of a new New Deal to rebuild the country, but Obama did not remind American citizens of his New Deal predecessor. That might have frightened the markets, but it would have educated citizens with short-term memories and raised hopes. Neoliberal politics did not encourage any such nonsense. Forbidden. Otherwise Obama could easily have educated the country on how it had dealt with similar problems under a previous Democratic administration. Following the crash of 1929, the Democratic Party went on the political offensive and created a new consensus in the country that survived till the Reagan years. In 1932, Roosevelt defeated Herbert Hoover on the basis of a reformist political program that won the support of the have-nots without breaching any systemic barriers. A flavor of those times is provided by the introduction to the Democratic platform of that year:

> In this time of unprecedented economic and social distress the Democratic Party declares its conviction that the chief causes of this condition were the disastrous policies pursued by our government since the world war, of economic isolation, fostering the merger of competitive businesses into monopolies and encouraging the indefensible expansion and contraction of credit for private profit at the expense of the public.
>
> Those who were responsible for these policies have abandoned the ideals on which the war was won and thrown away the fruits of victory, thus rejecting the greatest opportunity in history to bring peace, prosperity and happiness to our people and to the world.
>
> They have ruined our foreign trade; destroyed the values of our commodities and products; crippled our banking system; robbed millions of our people of their life savings and thrown millions more out of work; produced widespread poverty and brought the government to a state of financial distress unprecedented in time of peace.
>
> The only hope for improving present conditions, restoring employment, affording permanent relief to the people, and bringing the nation back to the proud position of domestic happiness and of financial, industrial and agricultural and commercial leadership in the world lies in a drastic change in economic governmental policies ... The Democratic Party solemnly promises by appropriate action to put into effect the principles, policies and reforms herein advocated, and to eradicate the policies, methods and practices herein condemned.

The New Deal was a product of its time. It did not appear from nowhere. Economic, social and political conditions were very different from today's. Militant trade unionism and factory occupations in defense of union rights on the domestic front, and abroad, a Europe becoming polarized between a still idealized Soviet Union and the communist idea and the fascism risen in Italy, Germany and Spain. Pressures from within and without pushed the Democrats in the direction of a new deal, though even their measures, which appear extremely radical compared to Obama's vapid formulas, did not succeed in revitalizing the economy. A renewed recession in 1937 was only ended by the industrial recovery generated by World War II.

An important New Deal legacy was the laws that provided some protection and some relief from corporate power and abuse. The 1933 Glass-Steagall Act was one such regulatory measure; it prevented investment banks from engaging in retail finance. Had this act not been finally repealed by the Clinton administration, there certainly would not have been a run on the investment and mortgage banks. In general, however, regulation is not always effective in dealing with corporate malfeasance because "as a rule, regulation is acquired by the industry and is designed and operated primarily for its benefit."[4]

By 2008, US trade unions were shrunken shadows of what they had been in the past. They had signed a Faustian pact with corporations and the state during the Cold War, a deal that retarded their effectiveness as workers' representatives.[5] Trade unions and corporations had collaborated on many levels since the fifties of the last century, especially, but not exclusively, in military industries, with joint lobbying efforts on behalf of the missile and more lately the drone industries. When tough trade unions were needed, few

4   George Stigler, "The Theory of Economic Regulation," quoted by Simon Johnson and James Kwak in *13 Bankers: The Wall Street Takeover and the Next Financial Meltdown*, New York, 2010, 93.
5   McCarthyism had proved effective in politically cleansing the unions and Hollywood, but only the latter recovered in time.

were available. The result was catastrophic for working people. When a new macroeconomic system, based on deindustrialization and deregulation, was imposed in the 1990s, the hopelessly compromised US unions, unlike their French and German counterparts and the social movements of South America, were in no position to resist the total corporatization of the economy. Even the most severe economic crisis does not automatically produce a radical shift in mass consciousness that challenges the dominant view. Capitalism is regularly faced with crises, the result of the deadly logic of an economy based on a state-buttressed market system. It has failed many times before but has usually recovered, including during periods when it confronted real political challenges. Its ability to adapt and survive should not be underestimated, even though it usually does so at the expense of the majority it exploits. In the twenty-first century the American ruling elite, confronting neither external nor internal pressures, feels no need to institute any structural reforms that regulate capitalism and benefit the majority of US citizens.

Until the emergence of a political movement with a viable sociopolitical and economic alternative perceived by a majority as such, there will be no final crisis of capitalism except in the dreams of those who desire something better. In order to save themselves, the global elites will consider approaches to the crisis that best preserve the status quo. The realistic choice they are faced with today is either to establish a public utility credit and banking operation geared to reviving a productive sector, or to shore up a discredited, deregulated Wall Street/City of London operation based on fictive capital. The latter option has prevailed.[6]

6   The lack of popular social movements in the United States enabled the elite to impose its own solutions, and these were, unsurprisingly, designed to boost the exist-

THE OBAMA SYNDROME

Obama is only too aware of this fact and is sometimes prone to use mass indifference as an excuse for his own opportunism. Would he like to be pushed in a more progressive direction from below, as many of his fans claim? His record suggests the opposite. Temperamentally, he is not a renovator but a conciliator. On the economy, each and every one of his appointments signaled no change to his Wall Street backers. Joseph Stiglitz, who at the very least might have forced the new administration to debate an alternative to the macroeconomic disaster that had occurred, was carefully sidelined. Lawrence Summers, one of the people responsible for the meltdown of 2008, was appointed head of the National Economic Council, as if to reward him for his prescience. It was he who pushed through the how-the-rich-can-get-richer legislation in November 1999—otherwise known as the Gramm-Leach-Bliley Act—that permitted the merger of commercial banks with investment banks, brokerages and insurance companies. Reading the funeral rites of the Glass-Steagall Act and embracing its replacement, Summers had this to say:

> Let me welcome you all here today for the signing of this historic legislation. With this bill, the American financial system takes a major step forward towards the twenty-first century, one that will benefit American consumers, business, and the

---

ing arrangements. The citizens in much of South America challenged deregulation and privatization more effectively than organized labor has done in North America or Western Europe. Similar actions in the US could have exerted pressure for a public, single-payer health service, massive investment in education, and reduced military spending, and against bailouts for the car industry and sinking airlines. Let them fall, should have been the demand, so that an ecologically sound and more efficient public transportation infrastructure can be built—especially a new railway system—that serves the needs of all. The lesson is an old one: without action from below, there will be no change above.

national economy for many years to come … I believe we have all found the right framework for America's future financial system.

A year later, the "right framework" could not prevent the collapse of dot-com shares. Greenspan had to drastically cut interest rates from 6.5 to 1 percent to keep the economy afloat and created a huge bubble based on cheap credit, provided largely by investors from China and Japan, that lifted property prices by 50 percent. But none of this worked. Fort Knox had been drained of reserves by the huge military expenditures necessitated by the wars in Iraq and Afghanistan and social spending at home. Meanwhile growth rates in the real economy continued to slide: 3.6 percent in 2004 to 0.8 in 2008.[7] One would think that all this might have pushed a newly elected president to search for new ideas and attempt a renovation of the system. As two insiders wrote:

> The challenges the United States faces are familiar territory to the people at the IMF. If you hid the name of the country and just showed them the numbers, there is no doubt what old IMF hands would say: nationalize troubled banks and break them up as necessary.[8]

Obama's choice of personnel suggested that he thought otherwise. Besides Summers, his appointees were Tim Geithner as the new sheriff at the Treasury and Neal Wolin as his deputy. As readers of

---

7 Compare Susan Watkins, "Shifting Sands," *New Left Review*, January/February 2010, 5–27.

8 Simon Johnson and James Kwak, "The Quiet Coup," *Atlantic*, May 2009. The same authors' book *13 Bankers* is a coldblooded survey of how bankers dominate the global economy and how finance capital is undermining democracy.

the *San Francisco Chronicle* were informed by Robert Scheer, all three were hardcore neoliberalizers:

> Wolin, Geithner and Summers were all protégés of Robert Rubin, who, as Clinton's treasury secretary, was the grand author of the strategy of freeing Wall Street firms from their Depression-era constraints. It was Wolin who, at Rubin's behest, became a key force in drafting the Gramm-Leach-Bliley Act, which ended the barrier between investment and commercial banks and insurance companies, thus permitting the new financial behemoths to become too big to fail. Two stunning examples of such giants that had to be rescued with public funds are Citigroup bank, where Rubin went to "earn" $120 million after leaving the Clinton White House, and the Hartford Insurance Co., where Wolin landed after he left Treasury.[9]

As late as 2006, Treasury Secretary Geithner had praised the innovations of the financial sector and suggested that they had "contributed to a substantial improvement in the financial strength of the core financial intermediaries and in the overall flexibility and resilience of the financial system of the United States … and in the increased stability in growth outcomes experienced over the past two decades."[10]

Pam Martens, who spent two decades working on Wall Street (and remains an informed critic of the system), makes it clear that Obama was leaving little to chance:

> Rounding out the list of those who got it wrong in the Clinton administration who have been brought back to get it wrong again in the Obama administration: Gary Gensler, one of those

9   "Where is the community organizer we elected?", *San Francisco Chronicle*, November 19, 2009.
10   Available online at ny.frb.org.

supporting the deregulation of derivatives under Clinton, now head of the Commodity Futures Trading Commission under President Obama; Gene Sperling, thanked by Lawrence Summers in the opening remarks at the signing of the legislation to repeal the Glass-Steagall Act, now counselor to Treasury Secretary Tim Geithner.[11]

The too little, too late "regulatory reforms" known as the Frank-Dodd Bill are virtually useless. As Robert Reich predicted they would, the Wall Street lobbyists won on the key issues at stake by allowing "secret derivative trading in foreign-exchange swaps (similar to what Goldman used to help Greece hide its debt) and in transactions between big banks and many of their corporate clients (as with AIG)."[12] A headline in the *Financial Times* expressed the collective sigh of relief heard from Wall Street in late June 2010 and signaled by a sharp rise in shares: "Bank stocks stage relief rally as cloud lifts." How could they not? The lobbyists had worked hard to remove any clause that might seriously damage Wall Street's divine right to speculate. Banks would carry on investing in hedge funds and private equity groups while retaining at least 70 percent of what is laughably referred to as the "derivatives business." The self-serving optimism of JPMorgan Chase, Goldman Sachs, etc., was not shared by mainstream economists: in the *New York Times*, party-pooper Paul Krugman predicted a depression as the inevitable result of the Federal Reserve and the European Central Bank opting to support credit markets in the face of catastrophic unemployment. In fact, the economic downturn is being used by corporations to sack employees as a way of increasing

---

11 Pam Martens, "Obama's Economic Brains Trust," *Counterpunch*, April 2–4, 2010.
12 Robert Reich, "Fraud in the Street," on his blog at robertreich.org.

profits and share prices: Caterpillar shares went up dramatically not because the company increased production and sales but because it fired 37,000 workers. When EU governments mimic these policies, they are merely delaying the crash.

Given the deep-rooted conservatism of the new administration, it was always foolish to expect anything substantial where it was most desperately needed: on the health care front. The situation here has long been a public scandal. The apparent paradox, as to how a country that in 2009 spent 17.4 percent of GDP (huge compared to Western Europe) on health care ends up with a sub-standard service that can't even compete with embargoed Cuba, is easily explained. Most of the money is spent on paying the corporations that dominate the medical industry. Current projections suggest that by 2011–12, the government share in health spending will exceed that of employers and individuals.[13]

Once upon a time, even Republican presidents, aware of the irrationality of this, tried to implement reforms to create a single-payer system. Richard Nixon's attempt to provide a system that benefited the public was defeated by the doctors' lobby. Subsequently, the late Edward Kennedy attempted to revive a version of the Nixon plan, without much success. The Clintons came up with a less attractive model. That, too, was mowed down by the corporate artillery of the medical-industrial complex. Numerous doctors and health specialists have been arguing for decades in favor of a single-payer system on the Canadian model. What would Obama do with his majority in the House and the Senate? The closer he came to winning the Democratic nomination, the

13   For a diagrammatic survey of comparative expenditure on health in the United States and Western Europe, see Appendix 3.

more his views on this issue began to shift. Proximity to power has an unsurprising ability to mutate a politician's spinal chord into bright yellow jelly.

On June 30, 2003, speaking to the Illinois AFL-CIO, Obama had been at his most radical, underlining the scandal of the state of health care in the country and arguing the case for universality:

> I happen to be a proponent of a single-payer universal health care program ... [*applause*] I see no reason why the United States of America, the wealthiest country in the history of the world, spending 14 percent of its Gross National Product on health care, cannot provide basic health insurance to everybody. And that's what Jim is talking about when he says everybody in, nobody out. A single-payer health care plan, a universal health care plan. And that's what I'd like to see. But as all of you know, we may not get there immediately. Because first we have to take back the White House, we have to take back the Senate, and we have to take back the House.

Five years later the Democrats had won all three, but no single-payer health service was in sight. Obama had already started to row backward on this one in 2006. In a lengthy interview with Joe Klein, he surprised even this ultra-friendly interlocutor by admitting that the dumping of "divisive" policies had already begun. Klein wrote:

> Universal health insurance also found its way to the cutting-room floor. I asked about the universal plan recently passed in Massachusetts, which was a triumph of Obama-style bipartisanship. The plan requires everyone who earns three times the poverty rate to purchase health insurance and subsidizes those who earn less than that. Shouldn't health insurance be mandatory, like auto insurance, for those who can afford it? Obama

wouldn't go there. "If there's a way of doing it voluntarily, that's more consonant with the American character," he said. "If you can't solve the problem without the government stepping in, that's when you make it mandatory."[14]

The final health care bill was a total capitulation to the "American character" and the insurance companies, the pharmaceutical giants, the for-profit hospitals and the top-of-the-market medical specialists. Lobbies favoring all three have numerous friends— Republican and Democrat—among lawmakers on Capitol Hill. And bribery is legal. And, it would seem, the White House approves. Obama pleaded with dozens of House Democrats who had agreed with his earlier position and had declared their intention to vote against what they regarded as an unnecessary compromise. In the event, they were all corralled into voting for the measure, but only after Obama had wooed them individually and said the vote was crucial because they had to pass something or else his presidency was on the line. This, at least, was a statement of fact. All of them, including Dennis Kucinich, caved. During the campaign Obama had boasted that he would prefer to be a one-term president rather than abandon his plans for change. This was never the case. From the first weeks after he was elected the second term was never far from his thoughts, and even an Obama-friendly *Los Angeles Times* was compelled to raise a few awkward questions:

> As a candidate for president, Barack Obama lambasted drug companies and the influence they wielded in Washington. He even ran a television ad targeting the industry's chief lobbyist, former Louisiana congressman Billy Tauzin, and the role Tauzin played in preventing Medicare from negotiating for

14 "The Fresh Face," *Time*, October 15, 2006.

lower drug prices. Since the election, Tauzin has morphed into the president's partner. He has been invited to the White House half a dozen times in recent months. There, he says, he eventually secured an agreement that the administration wouldn't try to overturn the very Medicare drug policy that Obama had criticized on the campaign trail.

"The White House blessed it," Tauzin said. At the same time, Tauzin said the industry he represents was offering political and financial support for the president's health care initiative, a remarkable shift considering that drug companies vigorously opposed a national overhaul the last time it was proposed, when Bill Clinton was president. If a package passes Congress, the pharmaceutical industry has pledged $80 billion in cost savings over 10 years to help pay for it. For his part, Tauzin said he had not only received the White House pledge to forswear Medicare drug price bargaining, but also a separate promise not to pursue another proposal Obama supported during the campaign: importing cheaper drugs from Canada or Europe. Both proposals could cost the industry billions, undermine its ability to develop new cures and, in the case of imports, possibly compromise safety, industry officials contend.[15]

In other words, the new president of the United States had ended up as a facilitator for the insurance and pharmaceutical industries. And as the distinguished scholar and practitioner Professor Arnold S. Relman of Harvard pointed out, not just for them alone. Health care had been monetized, transformed from a "community-oriented social system" into a huge industry and operated as such. What was at stake were

powerful vested economic interests ... who will resist and will have to be confronted ... All those investors who have an equity interest in a vast variety of for-profit health care businesses

15 Tom Hamburger, "Obama Gives Powerful Drug Lobby a Seat at the Healthcare Table," *Los Angeles Times*, August 4, 2009.

and all those medical specialists whose high income depends on the fee-for-service reimbursement of expensive technology and complex procedures will also have to be convinced that change is necessary before we make it to the promised land.[16]

Was there any choice? There was, but it was never taken up: it would have required breaking with the Reagan consensus. It would have meant a return to political campaigning; it would have involved transforming the 13 million Web-list supporters from virtual to real, mobilizing them to appear in public all over the land to debate, discuss and argue for a universal health care system. It could have culminated in a rally many millions strong in DC. In the president's lingo, there were asses that needed to be kicked. But a decision had already been taken not to buck the medical-industrial complex, and the promised health care reforms mutated into the slanted and abridged "health insurance reforms."

Why did Obama fail to challenge the town hall antics of his opponents—backed by corporate cash—who presented universal care as a challenge to individual freedom and opposed health care reform on principle? Here was an opportunity to take them on and reeducate the country. Instead he continued, in his characteristic presidential style, to try to unify opposites, using a language that effectively sealed off all other options. In the 1980s, over 70 percent of Americans believed that health care should be a constitutional right. In the decades prior to Obama's victory, opinion polls consistently revealed sizable majorities in favor of a unified health care system. An NBC/*Wall Street Journal* poll discovered that "two-thirds of all Americans thought that the government

16   Arnold S. Relman, "What to Do about Health Care," *New York Review of Books*, October 19, 2006.

should guarantee 'everyone the best and most advanced system that technology can supply.' " A rival survey conducted by the *Washington Post*/ABC uncovered the fact that 80 percent of Americans believed that universal health care was "more important than holding down taxes." Similar findings emerged in *Business Week*, and the Pew Research Center published a report stating that 64 percent of US citizens were in favor of guaranteed health insurance for every citizen, as in Canada and Britain.[17]

A weak, watered-down bill was finally pushed through, which expanded Medicaid to cover 16 million people on low incomes, but a great deal of confusion still exists as to what real impact this will have, and critics of various stripes were not mollified. One thing soon became clear. The administration had caved in to the antiabortionists by virtually outlawing federal funding of abortions: the pro-choice movement had been shafted by the very people it had supported. Sharon Lerner noted that even after the bill, groups like Emily's List, NARAL and Planned Parenthood's Action Fund,

> which score candidates according to their voting record on reproductive health issues, have decided not to include the final health care reform vote in scoring, a decision that reflects the fact that even their most loyal supporters in the House voted for the final legislation ... But, even with the antiabortion language, they couldn't judge the final vote the same way.[18]

17 Cited by Noam Chomsky, *Failed States: The Abuse of Power and the Assault on Democracy*, New York, 2006.
18 Sharon Lerner, "Nowhere to Hyde," *Nation*, April 1, 2010. Here was another example, if one was needed, of how a measure proposed by Obama was supported by "progressives" regardless of all else. Had this been a Republican bill, the pro-choice people might have been less restrained. Even the saintly Katha Pollitt, who watches every breach in women's rights with an eagle eye, was far too measured in her response.

And John R. Macarthur wrote in Britain's conservative *Spectator*:

> Given Obama's Windy City heritage, it is no surprise that his health care "reform" was written by Liz Fowler, a former executive for a private health insurer, who now works for Senator Max Baucus, the chairman of the Senate Finance Committee and a beneficiary of millions of dollars in contributions from insurance and health care companies.[19]

Clinton's former Labor Secretary, Robert Reich, now a professor at the University of California at Berkeley, was also critical and warned against spin-doctoring by advising people not to

> believe anyone who says Obama's health care legislation marks a swing of the pendulum back toward the Great Society and the New Deal. Obama's health bill is a very conservative piece of legislation, building on a Republican (a private market approach) rather than a New Deal foundation. The New Deal foundation would have offered Medicare to all Americans or, at the very least, featured a public insurance option.

Rose Anne DeMoro of the 150,000-strong National Nurses United described the passage of the bill as

> troubling for democracy, as is the pervasive corruption of corporate lobbying that so clearly influenced the language of the bill. As more Americans recognize the bill does not resemble the distortions peddled by the right, and become disappointed by their rising medical bills and ongoing fights with insurers for needed care, there will be new opportunity to press the case for real reform. Next time, let's get it done right.[20]

19 John R. Macarthur, "Under False Colours," *The Spectator*, May 5, 2010.
20 Rose Ann DeMoro, "On to Health Care Reform!", *Counterpunch*, March 25, 2010.

Obama's abject surrender to the insurance giants was bad enough. The failure to deal with the scandal that is the pharmaceutical sector was worse. Here we have a grotesque situation where corporations make a huge profit by selling overpriced medicines to the sick. In polar contrast, tiny Cuba produces most of the same medicines and provides them free to its citizens and extremely cheaply to the Caribbean, and Central and South America. Were the US to end the embargo, there is little doubt that millions of Americans would buy medicines from Cuba, in fact in even greater numbers than those who already order online drugs from Canada (currently estimated at two million plus).

The pharmaceutical giants, far removed from any meaningful regulation, have been expanding, aggrandizing themselves by mauling and swallowing smaller rivals in a display of greed that would shame a self-respecting shark. It is the most profitable industry in the United States. If ever any business needed a revolutionary change it is the one engaged in the production of medicines, the monster whose lobbyists control the legislature and to whom "Congress is so beholden ... that it will do its bidding at nearly any price."[21] This leads to "free-pricing and rapid approval," in the words of a pharma CEO. The cost to the state of paying absurdly inflated prices for drugs used by Medicare and Medicaid is becoming prohibitive. The trade in prescription drugs is unaffected by the recession. IMS Health forecast a 4 to 6 percent growth in 2010, increasing to 8 percent by 2014. The US market consumes half of the world's prescribed medicine, and in 2009 this amounted to sales of $300.3 billion.

21   Marcia Angell, MD, *The Truth About the Drug Companies: How They Deceive Us and What to Do About It*, New York, 2005.This is a sharp and thoughtful critique of a corruption for which no cures seem to be available.

The basic research in medicine and related technologies funded by US taxpayers is legally available to private companies who profit without fear and dispense favors to the powerful. This nexus of businessmen, politicians and senior doctors determines the future of the industry. The result is a classic example of capitalist irrationality. A non-profit, state-run pharmaceutical industry, for instance, would reduce costs to a minimum, provide prescription medicines free to those in need and cheaply to others, and if exported to the rest of the world these would have an immediate impact. Here the Cuban model that is being taken up by other South American countries would benefit North American citizens as well. Since the likelihood of any US politician favoring a state-controlled industry is remote, the import of cheap medicines from Cuba, Brazil or India would dramatically diminish expenditure in this field.[22] But since profits override health concerns, this, too, is unlikely to happen. Sadly, no political drug has yet been developed to cure the cancerous corruptions of US politics.

22　Even some of Cuba's enemies have been compelled to acknowledge its important successes in medicine. The Cubans have been extremely successful in producing vaccines, interferon and monoclonal antibodies. Sustained research on HIV/AIDS has produced an effective vaccine now being made available to the poorer countries around the globe. More than a decade ago, Dr. Vicente Verez, head of the University of Havana's Synthetic Antigens Laboratory, announced Cuban production of Haemophilus influenzae type b synthetic vaccine. The government believes that there should be no barriers to saving lives, and does not enforce patents. It produces a large supply of generic drugs that undercut the profit-obsessed pharmaceutical corporations of the West. This industry would benefit further if the Cubans went in for capitalism. When Cuban doctors arrive to help in emergency relief operations after natural disasters they bring their own equipment and medicines: their ability to train even illiterate peasants in basic hygiene and provide elementary medical training astonished earthquake victims in both Pakistan and Haiti. Had Obama been president during the New Orleans tragedy would he have accepted the offer of Cuban doctors that Bush declined?

In an affecting essay, Teri Reynolds, a young doctor working in Oakland, described the conditions that prevailed in the health sector that dealt with poor patients, conditions that the new bill will do little to rectify:

> I have been well aware of the fallout our imbalanced system has for county patients; but until recently I don't think I recognized the damage it was doing to the small minority it serves well. On one of my early shifts at the University of California hospital the triage nurse passed me a handwritten note from a patient in the waiting room. It read:
>
> "Please help me. My jaw has been broken and I am in a lot of pain. I've been here over an hour and am still bleeding. My hands and feet are numb and I'm starting to shake. I need some care. I have insurance."[23]

The jury on the new insurance reforms and their impact on health will be out for at least a decade, since the measures voted through will not be fully tested till 2019, by which time, even if reelected, President Obama will have moved on. His successor will have to deal with operational costs that will spin out of control, forcing new measures that will strip people of entitlements. The corporations, one can predict, will remain untouched.

The health of poor American citizens never did concern the corporations and the politicians they funded. What if a corporation were to openly destroy the ecological health of the country? "Drill, baby, drill" had been Sarah Palin's response to those who sought to defend the Alaskan coast from the deep-sea drilling and for which she was widely pilloried. What would happen to the guys who had authorized Deepwater Horizon?

23   Teri Reynolds's "Dispatches from the Emergency Room" was first published in the fiftieth anniversary issue of *New Left Review*, January/February 2010. For its exceptional quality, I have included it as Appendix 1.

In March 2010, flanked by Secretary of the Interior Ken Salazar, the president announced his decision to proceed with offshore drilling. The locale was carefully chosen: Andrews Air Force Base. This enabled him to dress up a tawdry merchandising decision in patriotic colors. He did not disappoint. His administration was considering new areas for drilling in the mid and south Atlantic and the Gulf of Mexico. He was aware, of course, that some "disagreed strongly" and there were even "those who say we should not open any new areas to drilling." He understood their concerns, but he was going to ignore them. He was not in favor of "drilling everywhere all the time" but had opted for a compromise solution while the search for alternative fuels carried on. Meanwhile it was time to introduce a new friend, the Green Hornet:

> Some of the press may be wondering why we are announcing offshore drilling in a hangar at Andrews Air Force Base. Well, if there's any doubt about the leadership that our military is showing, you just need to look at this F-18 fighter and the light-armored vehicle behind me. The Army and Marine Corps have been testing this vehicle on a mixture of biofuels. And this Navy fighter jet—appropriately called the Green Hornet—will be flown for the first time in just a few days, on Earth Day. If tests go as planned, it will be the first plane ever to fly faster than the speed of sound on a fuel mix that is half biomass ... Now, the Pentagon isn't seeking these alternative fuels just to protect our environment; they're pursuing these homegrown energy sources to protect our national security.[24]

24 "Remarks by the President on Energy Security at Andrews Air Force Base," March 31, 2010. In fact he should also have used the base to announce the insurance reform measures related to health care. The boost to insurance companies and the decision to leave the pharmaceuticals industry alone also involved the health of marines and other service people. And for another reason: the number of ex-military

In early April, to the delight of the oil and affiliated lobbies, Obama sent a proposal to Congress for increased offshore drilling:

> In the short term, as we transition to cleaner energy sources, we've still got to make some tough decisions about opening new offshore areas for oil and gas development in ways that protect communities and protect coastlines ... the bottom line is this: given our energy needs, in order to sustain economic growth and produce jobs, and keep our businesses competitive, we are going to need to harness traditional sources of fuel even as we ramp up production of new sources of renewable, home-grown energy ... We'll protect areas that are vital to tourism, the environment, and our national security. And we'll be guided not by political ideology, but by scientific evidence ... Ultimately, we need to move beyond the tired debates of the left and the right, between business leaders and environmental-ists, between those who would claim drilling is a cure-all and those who would claim it has no place. Because this issue is just too important to allow our progress to languish while we fight the same old battles over and over again.

Drilling industry prospects had not looked so good for decades. The unease created by the Exxon disaster in Alaska twenty-one years before had almost disappeared. On April 20, 2010, new sci-entific evidence was about to override the political ideology of the Obama administration. A BP rig exploded in the Gulf of Mexico, killing ten workers and spewing millions of gallons of oil into the sea. Two months after the explosion government experts announced that up to 30,000 barrels of oil were polluting the sea each day. It was the worst ecological disaster to have befallen the

---

officers working as salesmen for the giant pharmaceutical Pfizer is disproportionately high, as revealed in Jamie Reidy's *Hard Sell: The Evolution of a Viagra Salesman*, Kansas City, 2005.

country, and it was politician-made. The ideologues of deregulation and an unrestrained market were temporarily silenced by the image of oil-coated pelicans. The wrecked estuaries and marshes that sustain intricate ecosystems on the coastline of Louisiana suddenly revived the "tired debates" that the president had been so eager to forget. By late May, the oil had occupied the wetlands of the Mississippi river delta and was heading for the beaches and small islands in Vermillion Bay. A growing number of critics, including a few Democratic insiders, targeted the White House.

And for good reason. Both Obama and Ken Salazar had been strong proponents of deep-water drilling. During his four-year tenure as the senator from Colorado in 2005–9, Salazar had distinguished himself by his fulsome backing for Alberto Gonzales's nomination as Bush's attorney general during the confirmation hearings. It would be wrong to think that Salazar was uncritical of the Bush administration. He was extremely annoyed by the snail-pace drilling in the Gulf of Mexico and was one of the sponsors of the Gulf of Mexico Energy Security Act that made a further 8 million acres available for new drilling. His appointment as secretary of the interior was no accident. During the first twelve months of Obama's presidency, Salazar approved the lease of 53 million acres for a new surge in offshore drilling, overtaking, and with a vengeance, the record of the Bush administration.[25]

Obama had reacted slowly till he realized the scale of what had happened and, equally important, the growing public anger at the lack of activity on a federal level. Having ruled out preemptive regulatory strikes against the corporations, Obama subjected the CEO of BP to a severe tongue-lashing and was forced to suspend

25   Jeffrey St. Clair, "Oil Drilling under Clinton, Bush and Obama," *Counterpunch*, June 16–30, 2010.

his oil-drilling plan. The policies announced at Andrews Air Force Base were no longer operative. Deepwater Horizon had proved him wrong yet again. The confected rage was disingenuous. He threatened to force BP not to pay dividends till they had compensated workers and small businesses in the United States. The British prime minister pleaded on behalf of pensioners in his country whose funds had been invested in BP (another scandal, but part of the world in which we are forced to live), and the plan was dropped. Astonishingly, BP was allowed to carry on dealing with the spill when it was obvious that the government should have taken charge and made its main priority stopping the leak. Robert R. Reich had a better idea: "Wouldn't it be far simpler for the White House (stating that the Pollution Control Act of 1990 gives it authority) to put BP's American operations into temporary receivership? That way, Obama can take over BP's assets here and use its expertise to stop the leak and clean up the mess as soon as possible—and leave the subsequent years of bickering to the courts."[26]

One of the devices employed by political leaders in Europe and America since the Wall Street crash of 2008 has been to offload their own responsibility onto greedy bankers, receivers of obscene bonus payments and, in the case of the oil spill, to the bosses of BP, but the pride of corporate America, Halliburton, which was partially responsible for the rigs, was exempted from any blame. A servile corporate media, with few exceptions, monotonously promotes this view. It is individuals who are responsible, never the system that permits them to make these decisions, let alone the politicians (and not just those on the payroll of the corporation

26   Robert Reich, "Why the United States Can't Get BP to Do What's Necessary," guernicamag.com, June 13, 2010.

concerned) who authorize the policies that are considered repre-
hensible after a disaster.

In the aftermath of the Wall Street crash, individual CEOs were
the targets. The scale of the Gulf of Mexico disaster was so huge
that the entire company became the object of presidential wrath,
with another Democratic leader, Nancy Pelosi, demanding in
public that BP should not pay dividends to shareholders—which
include numerous British pension funds—till it had provided satis-
factory compensation to all those affected by the spill in the United
States. Fearful of the backlash, the politicians were trying to evade
their own responsibility for what had taken place. Once memories
of the latest spill have faded, which could be a long time, and once
the children are no longer asking questions, the drilling of the
seabed will quietly be resumed, or so the industry hopes. The
market capitalization for BP and the entire deepwater oil industry
may have fallen sharply, but it will recover in time. A change of
name (or a merger) from BP to GP might help, G standing for
Green and removing the linkage to any particular country.

Given the ecological record of the oil giants elsewhere in the
world, what happened in Louisiana should not have come as a
huge surprise. For a half century now environmentalists and con-
servationists have been highlighting the case of the Niger Delta in
Nigeria, which has suffered huge oil spills each year, totaling
several thousand, that have led to the deaths of animal life and
villages. The toxic mixture of poverty, pollution, company gang-
sterism and environmental degradation did not create an outrage
in the G8 world. One of the major offenders was BP. And deepwater drilling continues in other parts of West Africa. Politicians
in the African states are bought off easily by direct payments to
presidents and generals—there is no need to pay lobbyists and

incur overheads of the sort required to legally bribe US politicians from both parties. It was rage and despair that led local people inhabiting the polluted creeks and cities of the region to form MEND (Movement for the Emancipation of the Niger Delta) and launch a guerrilla war against the oil companies. They have succeeded in reducing the flow of oil by at least 40 percent.[27] The Niger Delta has yet to be cleaned up. Its people live in dire conditions. Perhaps the Gulf of Mexico disaster in the center of the world might indirectly help the periphery. Perhaps, when hell is gripped by permafrost.

Given the essential continuities between Obama's administration and previous ones on most other issues, it was extremely unlikely that education would prove to be an exception. As Clinton Democrats, they had already established a consensus with Bush on this issue many years ago. In the March 2001 issue of the Democratic Leadership Council's *Blueprint Magazine*, Andrew Rotherham had boasted that "Mr. Bush's education agenda is largely a New Democratic one ... The new education bill, which is regarded widely as 'Bush's education initiative,' was largely written by Democratic Sens. Joe Lieberman (Conn.) and Evan Bayh (Ind.), along with other New Democrats." The Democrats proudly accepted responsibility for the worst sections of Bush's "No Child Left Behind" measures. All of that would continue under Obama, but with some additions.

New Orleans was a newer model. As Hurricane Katrina lashed and finally broke through the levees in August 2005, destroying

27 For an excellent pictorial and written account of how the Niger Delta was wrecked, see *Curse of the Black Gold: 50 Years of Oil in the Niger Delta*, edited by Michael Watt and photographed by Ed Kash, Brooklyn, 2008.

schools as well as homes, offices and shops, the market fundamentalists detected an opportunity. One of the founding fathers of the movement, ninety-three-year-old Milton Friedman, still going strong, pointed out in the *Wall Street Journal*:

> Most New Orleans schools are in ruins, as are the homes of the children who have attended them. The children are now scattered all over the country. This is a tragedy. It is also an opportunity to radically reform the educational system.

Naomi Klein saw a pattern in this that she had detected in overseas imperial operations after heavy bombing and military occupation of sovereign states and that was, she argued, equally applicable at home after natural disasters. Privatization and corporate profits were the priority in rebuilding parts of battered Baghdad as well as New Orleans:

> Friedman's radical idea was that instead of spending a portion of the billions of dollars in reconstruction money on rebuilding and improving New Orleans' existing public school system, the government should provide families with vouchers, which they could spend at private institutions, many run at a profit, that would be subsidized by the state. It was crucial, Friedman wrote, that this fundamental change not be a stopgap but rather "a permanent reform."
>
> A network of right-wing think tanks seized on Friedman's proposal and descended on the city after the storm. The administration of George W. Bush backed up their plans with tens of millions of dollars to convert New Orleans schools into "charter schools," publicly funded institutions run by private entities according to their own rules ...
>
> In sharp contrast to the glacial pace with which the levees were repaired and the electricity grid brought back online, the auctioning-off of New Orleans' school system took place with

military speed and precision. Within 19 months, with most of the city's poor residents still in exile, New Orleans' public school system had been almost completely replaced by privately run charter schools. Before Hurricane Katrina, the school board had run 123 public schools; now it ran just 4. Before the storm, there had been 7 charter schools in the city; now there were 31. New Orleans teachers used to be represented by a strong union; now the union's contract had been shredded and its forty-seven hundred members had all been fired. Some of the younger teachers were rehired by the charters, at reduced salaries; most were not.[28]

So Friedman's advice was followed, and by the time he died, a year later, New Orleans schools had been effectively privatized and the local teachers union shredded. Where would market democracy strike next?

The present administration having failed to discover the grammar of a politics dedicated to the public good, it would have been a surprise if their "new" policies on education had turned out to be any different. The sub-Orwellian language of the Bush period had led to a federal law known as "No Child Left Behind," a mask designed to cover the fact that most children would be left behind under the new proposals, as they already had been under Clinton. At the very least, Obama should have consulted Diane Ravitch, whose credentials are impeccable. A registered Democrat, she served as Assistant Secretary of Education under Bush Sr. and as a member of the National Assessment Governing Board under Clinton, and is currently Professor of Education at New York University, with a reserved perch at the Brookings Institution.

28   *The Shock Doctrine: The Rise of Disaster Capitalism*, by Naomi Klein, New York, 2007, 5–6.

Her experience over the past few decades convinced her that the "reforms" that she had supported and whose implementation she had supervised were wrong, and that politicians and businessmen who pushed through "free market" policies in education were guided by motives other than that of improving the quality of public education. She questioned the constant use of the "reformer" tag attached to "those educators and officials who turned to market-based, data-driven reforms to produce higher scores." Invariably the very same people were deeply hostile to unions.[29]

Gradually Ravitch realized that none of the measures was working for the majority of the children and that the regime of continual testing, assessments and statistical evaluations was little short of a disaster. Meanwhile the new system was being praised to the skies for its punitive campaign against low-performing institutions, for closing down schools and boasting about it, creating a permanent sense of insecurity and helplessness in poor areas. Many teachers, in particular, complained bitterly of managerial bullying and a refusal to brook any challenge to the new system. The dictatorship of capital had reached the public schools. The charter schools so loved by the "school choice" gurus and favored by both Bushes, Clinton, and now Obama, are undemocratic insofar as they are unaccountable to elected officials and parents, and represent "a concerted effort to deregulate public education, with few restrictions on pedagogy, curriculum, class size, discipline, or other details of their operation."[30]

29　The failure of union leaders to pose a challenge to the "reformers" led to an astonishing upset in the 2010 leadership elections of the Chicago Teachers Union, when the traditional Democratic leadership, accused of collaboration, was defeated by a coalition of socialists. Their victory in the teeth of the inevitable red-baiting was an indication of grassroots anger.

30　Diane Ravitch, *The Death and Life of the Great American School System: How*

The privatization of schools proceeded apace, regardless of its odd crash on the West Coast, when the flagship California Charter Academy declared bankruptcy in 2004 at the start of the fall term, to the despair of the 6,000 students and their parents. The CEO, a former insurance company boss, had collected $100 million from state coffers to help fund his school business. The mechanics of the money machine were unfazed. As parents and teachers demanded a stop and threatened a referendum, Bill Gates donated a cool $1 million to sustain the supporters of "choice." Big money won the day, but the issues that were raised remain. One of these is extremely serious. It concerns the quality of education. The charter people and their backers have no educational vision. Their narrow-minded view of the world is imposed via market-driven curriculum changes. As Ravitch points out, countries as far afield as Japan and Finland that regularly outrank the US in mathematics and science have maintained a core curriculum that teaches arts, foreign languages, etc. This helps students to deal with ideas beyond the subjects in which they specialize.

Did anyone seriously brief Obama on the state of business-sponsored schooling? Was there any need to do so? Was the former senator from Chicago not aware that in neighboring Milwaukee the statistics revealed that the rich/poor, white/black disparities in education had been unaffected by the voucher program of the Clinton years? Even a casual reader of the *New York Times*, let alone the most literate president in recent memory, could not fail to notice reports of chicanery and corruption in this area. When the California Charter Academy collapsed, angry

---

Testing and Choice are Undermining Education, New York, 2010, 132–9. This first-rate book should be required reading for those who would imitate the US education system in Britain and elsewhere.

parents and teachers mobilized support against charter schools, though they faced stiff opposition. Bill Gates's donation was certainly made to save the program, not one academy. As the *Times* pointed out:

> When educational pioneers first began creating charter schools a decade ago, they provoked little controversy. But today, with 3,000 of the publicly financed, privately managed schools operating in 40 states, the subject has become one of the most contentious issues in education. Washington is not the only place to battle over charter schools recently. A Chicago plan to close 100 failing schools and replace some with charter schools has provoked protests. In Detroit, an entrepreneur offered $200 million to create 15 charter schools, but the teachers union and some parents persuaded the State Legislature to block the proposal. In Massachusetts and Ohio, school budget problems aggravated by the loss of money to charter schools have touched off a movement against them. Florida and California are tightening regulations after corruption scandals.[31]

In his first big speech on education after he became president, Obama assessed the situation:

> Despite resources that are unmatched anywhere in the world, we have let our grades slip, our schools crumble, our teacher quality fall short, and other nations outpace us … The relative decline of American education is untenable for our economy, unsustainable for our democracy, and unacceptable for our children. We cannot afford to let it continue. What is at stake is nothing less than the American dream.

---

31 Sam Dillon, "Voters to Decide on Charter Schools," *New York Times*, October 25, 2004.

The solution he offered was familiar. The market had to be brought in, and "charter schools" were praised as the need of the day. The fact that they had failed in so many parts of the country was considered irrelevant. Money has always talked big since the Reagan years, and Obama is no different from his predecessors.

Cometh the hour, cometh the man. Arne Duncan, responsible for the privatization of many of Chicago's schools and the dissolution of school councils (removing accountability altogether), was a veteran of the Chicago Democratic machine. Early on, Duncan, a product of private schools and with no teaching experience of his own, was a great believer in corporatizing education. He had assimilated a great deal of experience in that as a senior executive of Ariel Capital Management, whose brochure for their Potemkin school, Ariel Community Academy, read: "We want to make the stock market a topic of dinner table conversation." What better way to teach kids than by gifting first-graders with $20,000 to invest in a class stock portfolio? Each graduating class would return the original $20,000 to the new first grade and donate half the profits to the school, with the rest distributed among the graduates.[32] It has not yet been revealed whether any funds were invested in Ponzi schemes, or in Lehman Brothers or other dodgy companies. An Obama touch would be to have a voluntary extra class after church each Sunday, where kids could learn how regulation worked.

Arne Duncan moved on to become CEO of Chicago Public Schools. Together with Mayor Daley he hatched a fairly straightforward plan that probably originated at a Department of Defense worried by the fall-off in recruitment since the beginning of the

32   Adam Sanchez, "The Education 'Shock Doctrine,' " *International Socialist Review*, May/June 2010.

"war on terror." They agreed that some schools were to be made into naval and military academies to "offer the community more choice." When confronted by hundreds of teachers, parents and representatives of the local community concerned that the community school, Senn High, was being handed over to the Navy, Duncan understood their pain. How could he not? He was a genetic pacifist: "I come from a Quaker family, and I've always been against war. But I'm going to put the Naval Academy in there, because it will give people in the community more choices." Obama couldn't have put on a better display of hypocrisy himself and, clearly impressed, appointed Duncan as his Secretary for Education, simultaneously pleasing the military and the Chicago machine. Since 90 percent of the students in Chicago's public schools are nonwhite, what better choice for them than to be pushed in the direction of the armed services? In addition to helping out private companies, the plan was an ingenious device to permanently bypass the need for military conscription and to create a large pool of reserves, which might reduce the need for overpaid mercenaries from Blackwater and similar outfits.

The community schools in Chicago were not alone in their concern. The new proposals had disturbed a number of school principals elsewhere, who supported Obama on a number of issues but felt that the turn in education toward the market and competition as envisaged by the new administration was going to discriminate against low-income families. George Wood, the head of Federal Hocking High School in Ohio, confided his worries in an op-ed in the *Washington Post*. His argument was that the bulk of the funds were being made available to charter schools, and that the result might be to increase rather than decrease inequalities in education:

But we are not a charter school—thus, we are eligible for only slightly more than half the pool of federal money for innovation. Out of $900 million set aside for innovation, $400 million is designated for charter schools. Charters educate around 5 percent of the kids in our county, so why the largess? The Forum will call for innovation funds as well, but we want everyone—public and public charter schools—to have equal access to them.

At my school, we need more change than the Administration blueprint seems to be calling for. We need a greater emphasis on equity that guarantees for my students that their educational opportunities will not be based upon zip codes; we need teachers who are not only well-prepared and well-supported to teach in ways that are engaging and challenging, but who also do not have to sacrifice their financial well-being to work with our kids; we need to stop feeding the national culture of testing so we can establish a national culture of learning; and we need a fair and equal shot at all federal funds for innovation, regardless of what type of school we are.

Wood expressed the hope that the grotesque testing system would be reviewed, since it was unnecessary and wasted much time and energy that could be spent on real education, and that teachers would be genuinely helped:

> in my school, we have lost several great teachers because they could not make enough money to pay off student loans. Our teacher support programs, built around teacher leadership, professional development on-site, and common planning times for teachers who share students, are done with little or no support from the feds or the state.[33]

33 "A principal critiques Obama's education plan," *Washington Post*, March 18, 2010.

Wood and his colleagues should be more worried than they are. Teaching kids the art of financial speculation and war appears to be a priority for Duncan and the man who appointed him. They missed the odd trick: surely the CIA and FBI with their huge budgets should also be encouraged to set up academies and renew their gene pool.

The world of "accidental" judgments and casual slaughter, the palimpsest that is the secret state, grew from World War II onward through the Cold War and, most recently, the "war on terror." Though coupled with the accrual of virtually unlimited executive power in the name of a continuous emergency that has lasted since Pearl Harbor, it yet failed to prevent the assault on the Pentagon and Twin Towers; meanwhile, it induced the visible state to approve torture, imprisonment without trial, the slow death of habeas corpus, the horrors of Guantánamo, Bagram and Diego Garcia, until all these became as American as the once famous pie. So did the clichés justifying all of this in the media, clichés that grew legs of their own and went off on a world tour (while prisoners and wounded American soldiers were having their legs sawed off) and that needed a sharp rebuttal. What was Obama going to do about all this ugliness? On the campaign trail he had promised a return to the rule of law, but many in government regarded these emergency measures as the law. Obama reached out and embraced them without shame. To expect this president to prosecute members of the previous administration for crimes that were to be continued was truly utopian. He is an imperial president, and all those who run empires invariably commit crimes. Unsurprisingly, his new team spoke in familiar tones, much to the annoyance of venerable liberal historians:

At his confirmation hearing to be head of the CIA, Leon Panetta said that "extraordinary rendition"—the practice of sending prisoners to foreign countries—was a tool he meant to retain. Obama's nominee for solicitor-general [and now for the Supreme Court], Elena Kagan, told Congress that she agreed with John Yoo's claim that a terrorist captured anywhere should be subject to "battlefield law." On the first opportunity to abort trial proceedings by invoking "state secrets" … Obama's attorney-general, Eric Holder, did so. Obama refused to release photographs of "enhance interrogation." The CIA had earlier (illegally) destroyed ninety-two videotapes of such interrogations—and Obama refused to release documents describing the tapes.[34]

Rahm Emanuel, the White House attack dog, has referred to left-liberal critics of Obama as "fucking retarded." As panic grips the White House (a desperate president compares the self-inflicted Gulf of Mexico oil spill to 9/11), and as pro-Obama independent voters prepare to jump ship in droves (yes, they can), this might yet turn out to be an accurate self-description for the administration as a whole.

34   Garry Wills, "Entangled Giant," *New York Review of Books*, October 8, 2009.

117

4

SHERIFF OF THE WORLD

"I know thee, and thy dog and thy bush"
  Caliban, *The Tempest*, W. Shakespeare, 1611

"And thy seals!"
  Anon., 2011

1.

Domestic and foreign policies remain closely intertwined in the imperial United States.[1] Take for instance the campaign to reelect the president that began in earnest on May 2, 2011, with the revenge killing of Osama bin Laden in Abbotabad, a small, picturesque city in northern Pakistan, situated in the Himalayan foothills. The targeting and execution of America's Most Wanted

1 An optimistic view on how one might bring down the other can be read in a powerful essay by UCLA Professor Robert Brenner, in which he writes: "The American state is obsessed with building up and projecting military–political power, because power, and its expression, is available to it in no other manner or form. The US state builds its military strength, in a way, to compensate for its loss of economic power—and because it cannot rebuild this power—even though so doing will undoubtedly contribute to further relative economic decline and, in the end, political-military disintegration." Robert Brenner, "Why Bush Went to War," *New Left Review*, January/February 1991.

provided a dramatic start to the years ahead. A casually dressed president, his secretary of state, and military personnel watched the operation via a satellite link, looking like a scene from a Hollywood movie (which it undoubtedly will be, with Katherine Bigelow pumping the adrenalin). The cameras were ready in the East Room, and soon after the deed was done a statement from Obama was beamed to the world, achieving his highest audience figures ever: 56.5 million live viewers, on nine networks. Perfect figures, are they not, for launching the 2012 presidential campaign, provided the economy doesn't combust. The president, often criticized for being arrogant, disdainful, and solitary had suddenly become a perfect leader for a country at war.

And Obama was at his unctuous best as he stole the 9/11 imagery from his predecessor by providing some of his own: "And yet we know that the worst images are those that were unseen to the world. The empty seat at the dinner table. Children who were forced to grow up without their mother or their father. Parents who would never know the feeling of their child's embrace. Nearly 3,000 citizens taken from us, leaving a gaping hole in our hearts ..." The carefully crafted speech, a much better one than Bush could ever have made and almost on a par with some of Osama's sermons, ended like those of both, on a religious note: "Let us remember that we can do these things not just because of wealth or power, but because of who we are: 'one nation, under God, indivisible, with liberty and justice for all.' Thank you. May God bless you. And may God bless the United States of America."

And God did, as he so often does, and so did the global media networks that switched over, without any sense of unease, from celebrating a royal wedding in London to exulting over a kill-mission in Pakistan. The wedding was designed to rebrand the English monarchy; the killing did the same for President Obama. As if on cue, cheering crowds appeared on the streets in DC and New York to rejoice in the deed. European and other leaders (including, bizarrely, the prime minister of Pakistan) queued on the White House phone to offer congratulations.

Not a few liberals approved the style and technique of the killing in Abbotabad, gushing over the technical aspects of the great triumph and, in particular, the wondrous performing Navy Seals. Gary Wills, professor of history emeritus at Northwestern, whom I mentioned in the preceding chapter as expressing serious concerns about Obama's pitiful record on civil liberties, was back on track, energized by Osama's execution. For him the event proved conclusively that Obama was not "flaccid or feckless on national defense and military action," as alleged by the Republican right and, therefore, it was important that, while admiring the "superb things done by our Navy Seals … we should keep somewhere in the back of our minds a remembrance that the one ultimately pulling the trigger in both Seal actions was the President of the United States."[2]

From her *New York Times* perch, Maureen Dowd, mildly critical of Obama in the past, was now in raptures:

> No wonder the president's top generals call him "a Cool Hand Luke." If we could have seen everything unfolding in real time, it would have had the same dramatic effect as the intercutting in the president's favorite movie, *The Godfather*, when Michael Corleone calmly acts as godfather at his nephew's baptism at church, even as his lieutenants carry out the gory hits he has ordered on rival mobsters.

2   *NYRB* blog, May 6, 2011.

> Just substitute "Leave the copter, take the corpse" for "Leave the gun, take the cannoli."

She loved "the president's studied cool and unreadable mien." They may have been inappropriate on other occasions, distancing him from ordinary citizens, "but in the long-delayed showdown with Public Enemy No. 1, these qualities served him perfectly." She concluded with a rousing call to arms couched in language normally associated with those regarded by her ilk as "public enemies": "I want memory, and justice, and revenge … Liberal guilt may have its uses, but it should not be wasted on this kill-mission. Morally and operationally, this was counterterrorism at its finest. We have nothing to apologize for."[3]

Unsurprisingly, Obama's role was much appreciated by his predecessor and, a bit more grudgingly, by two members of his predecessor's team: Dick Cheney and Donald Rumsfeld. The latter had no doubts that information revealed by the torture used in Guantanamo had helped track the victim. It was left to a conservative columnist to draw attention to a fact that liberal apologists for the White House prefer to ignore.[4]

And it was Steve Bell, the inimitable political cartoonist at the *Guardian* in London who expressed a wider view. Bell, too, recalled *The Godfather*, but in a somewhat different register (see frontispiece).

---

3 Quoted by Alexander Cockburn in his biting *Counterpunch* Diary on the same theme, May 13–15, 2011.

4 "For those with eyes to see, the daylight between the foreign policies of George W. Bush and Barack Obama has been shrinking ever since the current president took the oath of office. But last week made it official: When the story of America's post-9/11 wars is written, historians will be obliged to assess the two administrations together, and pass judgment on the Bush-Obama era," Ross Douthat, "Whose Foreign Policy Is It?" *International Herald Tribune,* May 10, 2011.

Many young American liberals rushed out into the streets to celebrate Osama's assassination. At Ground Zero, as a blogger for the radical literary magazine *N+1* reported, the crowd was chanting, "U-S-A. U-S-A / Obama got Osama. Obama Got Osama / You can't beat us (clap-clap-clap-clap-clap-clap) You can't beat us / Fuck bin La-den. Fuck bin La-den." The blogger and his girlfriend, like the others, had rejoiced. As he wrote: "… I am glad that this man, this TV character dressed up like a thirteenth-century shepherd with a prop AK-47, is dead. I am glad he is dead I am glad he is dead." Civilization is only skin-deep. Contrast this blogger's attitude with that of Frank O'Connor, a former New York firefighter who expressed his disquiet with dignity:

My heart screams, "You sonofabitch, rest in pieces." But as a Vietnam vet, and a 62-year-old man who has seen firsthand suffering and death, I was troubled at the hairless faces swelling in the streets chanting, "U.S.A., U.S.A." If you wear the other man's caftan, one man's terrorist becomes another man's patriot.

What if an Iraqi assassinated George W. Bush and then screamed "justice" while Arabs danced in the streets? When Muslims dance over our misfortune, we're repulsed. Similar reactions by Americans send the wrong message throughout the Arab world.

This isn't a sporting event. These inappropriate celebrations violate human dignity, and the inherent sanctity of human life. Celebrating death, even an enemy's, reminds me of the anger I felt at seeing Afghans dancing in the streets the day the Towers fell. Veterans and firefighters have no monopoly on graphic, agonizing memories, but men in uniform are painfully aware that casualties have faces, lives and stories. Numbers can be adjusted, or corrected, people can't. Bones shatter; blood spills and limbs detach. The words "rescue worker dead" flow easy from a commentator's well-paid lips. But someone who

> compresses his comrade's head to prevent his brain from sliding
> into the desert sand won't describe death so casually ...[5]

The general triumphalism also ignored the disastrous results of the
"war on terror" at home and abroad. There was no mention, naturally, of the million "empty seats at dinner tables" in Iraq, where
the figures provided by the current regime speak of five million
orphans. Not a word of regret for them or the two million Iraqi
refugees. No mention either of the almost 2,000 civilian deaths
caused by Obama's drone attacks in Pakistan, or of the deaths of
innocents in Afghanistan—three times the number of those killed
on 9/11.

Saner voices from within the military and academic establish-
ments have been patiently trying to explain all this, but to no avail.
Obama, like his predecessors, is caught in the imperial rut. In April
2009, retired Colonel Douglas Macgregor said, "The most important choice President Obama must make is to reject future,
unnecessary, large-scale, overt military interventions in favor of
conflict avoidance" and went on to write in the *Armed Forces Journal*:

> Despite the seriousness of the present economic crisis, the
> greatest danger to American National Security is Washington's
> inclination to impose political solutions with the use of
> American military power in many parts of the world where
> Washington's solutions are both unneeded and unsustainable.
> President Obama must arrest this tendency by making prag-
> matic and methodical changes to the goals of American military
> strategy. In both Iraq and Afghanistan, America's military action
> has already produced disastrous consequences for US national
> security interests; namely,

5 William O'Connor, "No Time for Dancing in the Streets," *Counterpunch*, May
12, 2011.

- the expansion of Iranian regional power in Iraq and the Middle East,
- the alienation of Turkey, the Middle Eastern state with the most powerful military establishment in the region,
- the erosion of Pakistan's fragile cohesion with dangerous implications for all of Central and Southwest Asia,
- a more vulnerable Israeli State,
- a global anti-American backlash, and,
- declining American economic performance.

Two years later, John Mearsheimer, one of the country's most distinguished realist thinkers, linked the wars abroad to the assault on civil liberties at home, a thought that had not occurred to Professor Wills or Mo Dowd:

> The United States has been at war for a startling two out of every three years since 1989, and there is no end in sight. As anyone with a rudimentary knowledge of world events knows, countries that continuously fight wars invariably build powerful national-security bureaucracies that undermine civil liberties and make it difficult to hold leaders accountable for their behavior; and they invariably end up adopting ruthless policies normally associated with brutal dictators.

He reminded a nation that often mistakes media sound bites for history that:

> The Founding Fathers understood this problem, as is clear from James Madison's observation that "no nation can preserve its freedom in the midst of continual warfare." Washington's pursuit of policies like assassination, rendition and torture over the past decade, not to mention the weakening of the rule of law at home, shows that their fears were justified.[6]

6 John J. Mearsheimer, "Imperial by Design," *The National Interest* (January–February, 2011).

Obama was not interested in such talk. Emboldened by the response to his first big "triumph," he struck a tough note three weeks later, warning that when the US went hunting for terrorists, Pakistan's sovereignty was irrelevant; if necessary, the US would act so again. One assumes that a few more kills closer to November 2012 would seal his reelection.

What made the hollowing out of democracy in its Western heartland all the more ironic was a far more significant development, one that began in January 2011, had already marginalized an increasingly insignificant al-Qaeda and its elderly, retired, late leader. And much else besides. After the defeat inflicted by Israel and its backers on Arab nationalism in 1967, the great bard of that world, the late Nizar Qabbani, wrote:

> Arab children,
> Corn ears of the future,
> You will break our chains.
> Kill the opium in our heads,
> Kill the illusions.
> Arab children,
> Don't read about our suffocated generation,
> We are a hopeless case,
> As worthless as a watermelon rind.
> Don't read about us,
> Don't ape us,
> Don't accept us,
> Don't accept our ideas,
> We are a nation of crooks and jugglers.
> Arab children,
> Spring rain,
> Corn ears of the future,
> You are the generation that will overcome defeat.

The opening months of 2011 would have pleased Qabbani's heart, as the much-maligned Arab street resounded to the shouts of the masses: "Al-Sha'b yurid isquat al-nizam!"—"The people want the downfall of the regime!" The images streaming out from Tunis to Cairo, Saana to Bahrain were of the Arab peoples rising from their knees once again. On January 14, as chanting crowds converged on Tunisia's Ministry of the Interior, President Ben Ali and his family fled to Saudi Arabia. On February 11, the national uprising in Egypt toppled the dictatorship of Hosni Mubarak, while mass rebellion erupted in Libya and Yemen. In occupied Iraq, demonstrators protested against the corruption of the Maliki regime. Jordan was shaken by nationwide strikes. Protests in Bahrain spiraled into calls for the overthrow of the monarchy. And soon, the corrupt and brutal Baathist outfit in Syria was under siege by the Syrian people.

The patchwork political landscape of the Arab world—client monarchies; degenerated nationalist dictatorships; imperial petrol stations, a.k.a. the Gulf States—was the outcome of an intensive historical experience of Anglo-French colonialism. After the Second World War, the old colonial powers were replaced by a complex process of imperial transition, by the United States, and the results were a radical anti-colonial Arab nationalism and Zionist expansionism, both developing within the wider framework of the Cold War. When the Cold War ended, Washington took complete charge of the region, initially through local potentates and subsequently via military bases and direct occupation. Democracy never entered the frame, enabling the Israelis to boast that they and they alone were an oasis of light in the heart of Arab darkness. How has all this been affected by the Arab Spring?

The determinants of the uprisings have been both economic—

mass unemployment, rising prices, scarcity of essential commodities —and political: cronyism, corruption, repression, and torture. Egypt and Saudi Arabia were the crucial pillars of US strategy in the region, as confirmed by Vice President Joe Biden, who stated that he was more concerned about Egypt than Libya. The worry here is over Israel: the US fears that an out-of-control democratic government in Egypt might renege on a "peace treaty" whose principal function was to isolate Palestine and its people. Washington has, for the time being, succeeded in rerouting the political process into a carefully orchestrated change from above, led by Mubarak's defense minister and chief of staff—the latter is particularly close to the Pentagon. The bulk of the regime is still in place. Its key messages are the need for stability and a return to work—putting a stop to the wave of strikes and labor mobilizations. Fevered behind-the-scenes negotiations between Washington and the Muslim Brotherhood are designed to prevent any serious shift in Egypt's relations with Israel. A slightly amended old constitution remains in force, and the South American model of huge social movements producing new political organizations that triumph at the polls and institute social reforms is hardly being replicated in the Arab world; there has been no serious challenge there, so far, to the economic status quo. The mass movement remains alert in both Tunisia and Egypt but is short of political instruments that reflect the general will. The first phase is over. The second, that of rolling back the movements, has begun.

The unrelenting NATO bombing of Libya was little more than an attempt by Western powers to regain the "democratic" initiative after their dictators were toppled elsewhere. It has made the situation worse. This so-called preempting of a massacre has led to the killing of hundreds of Libyan soldiers, many of whom were fighting under duress, and permitted the ghastly Gaddafi to masquerade as an "anti-imperialist." Here one has to say that whatever the final outcome, the Libyan people have lost. The country will either be partitioned (a favored imperial ploy) into a Gaddafi-led state and a squalid pro-West protectorate led by selected businessmen, or else the West will take out Gaddafi and control the whole of Libya and its huge oil reserves. This display of affection for "democracy" does not extend to any other country in the region.

In Bahrain, the United States clearly green-lighted a Saudi military intervention to preserve the local despot, crush the movement for democracy, enhance religious sectarianism, and organize secret trials and sentence protestors to death. Bahrain today is a prison camp, a poisonous mixture of Guantanamo and Saudi Arabia where pogroms against the Shia majority are in progress. In Syria, the Baathist security apparatus led by the Assad family is shooting and killing at will, but without being able to crush the democratic movement. The opposition is not under the control of Islamists. It is a broad coalition that includes every social layer in the country apart from the capitalist class that has remained loyal to the regime. Unlike their counterparts in other Arab countries, many Syrian intellectuals stayed at home, suffering prison and torture, and secular socialists like Riad Turk and many others are part of the underground leadership in Damascus and Aleppo. Nobody wants Western military intervention. They don't want a repeat of Iraq or Libya. The Israelis and the US would prefer Assad to stay on the "better the devil you know" principle, but here the dice might remain in the air for some time to come.

Given the strategic importance assigned to the region by successive US presidents regardless of their party affiliation, a brief history of the intensity of imperial domination of this region might not be out of order. This is the first time since the mid-twentieth century that a wave of uprisings has crossed national borders with ease and swept the entire region from Tangiers to Tehran, reawakening memories in the Arab world of a unified nation.

But the character of this Arab wave is obviously also quite specific. Any attempt to grasp its full meaning would have to include an exploration of the particular dynamic of each national instance, but these also need to be understood in terms of the Arab world's location within the international order as a whole. For the notion of an "Arab world" does not rest solely on commonalities of culture, language, and religion—let alone, in a region that embraces Berbers, Tuaregs, Numidians, Persians, Kurds, and many others, any ethnic basis. It has also been shaped by a series of Western interventions more intensive than anywhere else on the globe. Anglo-French colonialism carved nearly two dozen states and statelets from the outskirts of the Ottoman Empire between 1830 and 1945, skewing local economies to the needs of colons or the metropolis. This was followed by US hegemony, operating in the context of the Cold War and underwriting, at the moment of decolonization and independence, the new settler-colonial state of Israel, while asserting control over access to Gulf oil as a "vital national security interest." Its control of the region was, however, not complete. The existence of the Soviet Union as a countervailing force in world politics provided some space for genuine independence, and Nasser's Egypt made full use of this fact. The Soviet collapse and the end of the Cold War altered the picture once again. The Middle East has borne the brunt of successive American military interventions—over a million civilians have been killed there since 1990. Meanwhile the European Union, with US backing, took upon itself the task of restructuring the Maghreb states.

In the first phase of this history, Anglo-French penetration, Britain concentrated its attention on Egypt, the Arabian Peninsula and the Persian Gulf—the route to India. The Egyptian monarchy was kept in place, entangled in debt, while the state was run by London. In the Gulf, local families were pressed to sign away their external rights in exchange for protectorate status; the Khalifas of Bahrain, Thanis of Qatar, Sabahs of Kuwait, and Qaboos of Oman owe their thrones to the Royal Navy. France focused on the western Maghreb: planting settlers in Algeria, where the local population was reduced by half, and retaining as clients the local rulers in Morocco and Tunisia, where—as in Egypt—the bey's modernization program had left him indebted to French banks. The Libyan provinces were reserved for particularly brutal subjugation to Italy, under Badoglio and Mussolini. After 1918, London and Paris carved out the states of the modern Middle East, famously using their self-awarded mandates to "prepare for independence" as a means of instituting colonialism-on-the-cheap. Britain transplanted client monarchs from Mecca to Transjordan and Iraq, sanctioned the House of Saud's conquest of Arabia, carved out the micro-kingdom of Kuwait, furthered Zionist immigration into Palestine, and crushed the 1936–1939 Arab revolt. North of the Sykes-Picot line, France operated a divide-and-rule policy among the mixed-faith populations: ring-fencing a Christian-led statelet in Lebanon and promoting minorities to run the Syrian security services. Arab armed forces were kept small—France reduced Syrian troop strength from 7,000 to 2,000—and would prove incapable of resisting the heavy armor assembled by Haganah's international backers in 1948.

This was the typical legacy for the Arab states at independence: a weak, collaborationist monarch—in Egypt, Tunisia, Iraq, Jordan, and Libya, where the British installed a Sanusi leader as King Idris I after capturing the Italian colony during the Desert War—who presided over a political system dominated by conservative notables, and traditional religious and administrative structures that were decaying but largely intact. More dynamic social forces—modernizing national bourgeoisies, rising middle strata, embryonic labor movements—would be obliged to overthrow these relics. Junior officers had both the means and the will to do so, and military coups established the regimes of Nasser in Egypt, Qasim in Iraq, Shishakli in Syria, and Gaddafi in Libya, initially with broad popular support. In Algeria, an eight-year insurgency exhausted the independence movement as much as it did the French, but Boumédiene's army remained intact and moved to install Ben Bella in 1962. Only in Morocco, where the French had made a national hero of the king by exiling him, and on the Arabian Peninsula, never directly colonized apart from the British base at Aden, would conservative monarchies persist.

But with independence still on the horizon, the region was subjected to two further interventions, announcing the arrival of a new imperial order under a capitalist power vastly stronger than the British or French. First came Eisenhower's 1943 declaration that Saudi oil would be considered "vital to American security interests." Second, with tacit American supervision, Zionist forces undertook the same process that Bureau had carried out in Algeria and Badoglio in Libya: militarized expropriation of Palestinian land and villages for colonial settlement. Oil and Israel have been the two unalterable determinants of US policy in the region ever since. Yet American strategy was not just imperialist. It was also hegemonic: aiming to win nonaligned Arab states for the West and roll back Soviet influence. The decisive moment here came in October 1973: both the high point of Arab unity and its nemesis. In a matter of days, Egypt sliced through the IDF occupation force east of the Suez Canal and Syria retook its lost land on the Golan Heights. Backed by a Saudi-led OPEC threat to cut oil production, they demanded that Israel pull out of the Palestinian territories it had occupied since 1967. Within a week, a massive US airlift of arms to Israel reversed the course of the war, leaving the Egyptian Third Army encircled in the desert. That army could only look to Washington for its salvation, and Kissinger seized the chance to lock the leading Arab state into the US order. During the five years of step-by-step diplomacy that followed, Sadat made one concession after another—ending the oil embargo, opening markets to US capital, excluding the PLO from talks, endlessly deferring a Palestinian settlement—and in return the Israelis would retreat a few miles back across the vastness of the Sinai desert. The treaty, finally signed in 1979, proved not so much a peace agreement as a license for unilateral war: Egypt retained its army, but surrendered the ability to use it, and with Arab power neutralized, Israel redoubled its arsenal, invaded Lebanon, put down the Palestinian intifada, and agitated for attack on Iraq and Iran.

It is widely thought that a third phase opened after 1990, when the end of the Cold War enabled the untrammeled use of US military force across an arc of conflict that now stretches from the eastern Mediterranean to the Hindu Kush. With Operation Desert Storm there began a huge advance of American troops and hardware into the Arabian peninsula, an expansion of naval bases in the Gulf and Arabian Sea and a decade of bombing raids on Iraq, followed, after the blowback of 9/11, by occupations of

Afghanistan and Iraq, penetration into Pakistan, and military aid and armed drones for Saleh in Yemen. The 1990s brought a new dawn for dictatorships in the Arab world. Elsewhere authoritarian rule was giving way to parliamentary representation, but here the political landscape was frozen into place. Pro-Western regimes were cosseted with American aid, and their spy systems and torture chambers were integrated into US and EU networks; meanwhile, "secular" holdouts like Algeria and Syria were tacitly supported as bulwarks against Islamism. A culture of impunity spread from the top.

It was within this darkening post-1990 regional context that the Arab world's social and economic outcomes diverged downward from those of Latin America and Southeast Asia—to which in the 1960s and 70s they had favorably compared. At independence, the legacy was of largely rural economies, with impoverished sub-proletariats created—in Egypt, in Algeria—where colonial powers had expropriated land for commercial use. State-led investment, industrial expansion and modest land reform brought a boom period in the first decades of independence, boosted by windfall oil rents in the 1970s. By the mid 1980s, oil prices had plummeted and growth petered out. The globalization boom passed the Arab world by: Turkey and Egypt, each with a population of 80 million, had roughly equal GDPs through to the mid 1970s. By the early 1990s, Turkey's growth rate was four times higher and since 2001 it has soared ahead: in 2008 Egypt's GDP was $162 billion and Turkey's was $730 billion. IMF and World Bank solutions—tariff-cutting, privatization, free capital flows, plus a shift from agriculture and manufacturing to services and tourism—helped foster gilded elites of regime insiders. Population growth swelled the region's numbers from 150 million in the 1970s to 300 million today, with a huge youth bulge—some 50 per cent of the populace is under twenty-five, densely concentrated on the coasts, the Nile Valley and the banks of the Levantine rivers.

In Tunisia, the origins of the current uprising were clearly social, beginning in the agricultural towns of the interior, where anger has been boiling over rising living costs, high unemployment and dead-end lives. Sidi Bouzid—where Mohamed Bouazizi set himself alight on December 16, in protest against police extortion and the expropriation of his only means of livelihood, a vegetable stall—is a town of around 30,000, left high and dry by the EU-led restructuring from the '90s, which tilted the economy toward coastal services, real estate, and tourism, while agriculture was undermined by cheap wheat imports. The only form of social security was an expanded secondary-school system; the cohort born in the 1980s, just as the post-independence boom collapsed, produced a generation of Mohamed Bouazizis, with bachelor's degrees but no prospects of jobs or marriage. He was the third young man to immolate himself in 2010.

Clashes between youth and police escalated as they spread, between December 19 and January 5, from Sidi Bouzid to Menzel, Bouzaiene, and Meknassy, with mass arrests fueling ever larger protests; then to the depressed phosphate-mining region of Metlaoui, Kasserine, and Thala. Al-Jazeera—whose sponsor, the Emir of Qatar, has been at loggerheads with Ben Ali—gave extensive coverage to the protests, relaying footage uploaded from demonstrators' phones. Spurred by images of police opening fire at Kasserine, the hitherto working-class revolt leapt to the major cities, mobilizing the middle class in Tunis, Sfax, and Muntasir, and took on political form: first the ousting of the interior minister, then the toppling of the regime. The national trade-union federation UGTT was faced with internal revolt; after long years of collaboration, it finally authorized general strikes, on January 11. At the same moment, the chief of staff declared that the army would not open fire on the people. He was promptly sacked by Ben Ali. From January 12, hundreds of thousands of people converged on the Ministry of the Interior, calling for the downfall of the regime. Popular anger was unleashed against the symbols of the Ben Ali–Trabelsi family's wealth, fruit of the French-led privatization program. The army moved to secure key government buildings and—crucially—faced down the presidential guard. On January 14, Ben Ali and his family fled to Riyadh.

The Tunisian army had always kept itself at arm's length from the regime. It played a marginal role in the independence struggle against the French, led by Bourguiba's powerful Neo-Destour Party, which combined support from the big bourgeoisie with a broad petty bourgeois and trade union base. France relinquished control in 1956, to concentrate on the defense of its Algerian possessions. There was no armed struggle; the bey was deposed in 1957 by parliamentary vote. The military remained on the sidelines, while the party—its name changed to RCD in later years —became a megalithic force, with two million members in a country of ten million. Ben Ali, a former Sûreté Nationale chief, eased the aged Bourguiba aside in 1987, having made his name as interior minister by crushing the nascent Islamists the previous year. As president, Ben Ali expanded the police force but kept the army, only 35,000 strong, at a distance. Since January 14 the army has been present on the streets, along with a much-depleted police force, but at the level of state power, it remains behind the scenes.

After the dictator's flight, his ministers attempted to cling to power, recruiting figures from the official opposition—Najib Chebbi of the liberal Progressive Democratic Party; Ahmed Ibrahim of the Ettajdid movement, the ex-CP—to "broaden" the government, with the speaker as interim president. But the mass movement continued to mobilize, both in the coastal cities and the interior. A Council for the Protection of the Revolution was constituted by Nahda, the Islamist party banned under Ben Ali, the UGTT, left-wing groups, and independent radicals, all demanding a break with the old regime. Nahda's leader, Rachid Ghannouchi, had been met at the airport by a crowd of 10,000 on his return from exile. The Council established a permanent camp outside the National Assembly building, a focus for further mobilizations and wide-ranging debates. In the interior, protests erupted when newly appointed provincial governors turned out to be familiar RCD figures. On March 4, the Council for the Protection of the Revolution succeeded in getting the old prime minister sacked. He was replaced by a veteran Bourguiba-era figure, Beji Caid Sebsi, who denounced the Ben Ali regime as saboteurs and announced forthwith the abolition of the state security apparatus, the dissolution of the RCD and the liquidation of its assets, and the appointment of commissions to investigate corruption, institute political reform, and establish human rights. Ben Ali's interior minister, Kacem, was charged with murder, and warrants were issued for the arrest of Ben Ali and Ali's wife.

The situation on the ground remains confused. In the interior —Kasserine, Sidi Bouzid, El Kef—there have been reports of RCD leaders, government officials and local businessmen instigating looting and arson attacks as cover to destroy files in police and government offices, while the army stands by. Yet following angry confrontations between local citizens and the military, Tunis has sent higher-ranking officers who ordered that the ringleaders of these exploits be detained for questioning.

The Constituent assembly elections on July 24 will give a clearer picture of the political balance of forces. In Egypt, social problems loom still larger: a fifth of the population is concentrated in greater Cairo; labor conditions are precarious, housing shortages are severe. Remittances from the Gulf fell precipitously during the global recession; in 2008, food-price rises sparked riots. Even so, the focus of the January 25 Coalition was initially political: it called for repeal of the Emergency Law; the ousting of Interior Minister Adli; and, after police repression was unleashed against the protesters in Tahrir Square, for the downfall of the regime. Shaken by events in Tunisia, the White House was intensively involved in trying to micromanage the outcome in Egypt almost from the start, Obama and Clinton insisting that Mubarak, who had crushed the people under his heel for thirty years, "must not be humiliated." The young radicals of January 25—the April 6 Movement, liberals, left-wing groups, Muslim Brotherhood youth—were resolute in facing down the Obama administration's attempts to corral the protesters into negotiations under Mubarak's intelligence chief, Omar Suleiman. They insisted, "No negotiations until he's gone." Washington was obliged to retreat, step by step, under pressure from the mass movement, backing first an "orderly transition," with Mubarak stepping down in September, then a handover to the torturer-in-chief, Omar Suleiman, and finally—amid cries of "Traitor!" from Riyadh and Tel Aviv— urging the Supreme Military Council into action, with Mubarak's February 11 departure preannounced to Congress by the head of the CIA. Washington ensured that the SMC's first act was to affirm its commitment to "all external agreements": the 1979 Treaty, subsidized gas sales to Israel, and free passage through the Suez Canal for Israeli nuclear submarines and for US aircraft carriers heading for service over Iraq and Afghanistan.

The army has been a central pillar of the Egyptian ruling order since the Free Officers' coup in 1952; since 1979, it has looked to the Pentagon for its training, weapons, and pay. Close collegial relations between Egypt's top generals and the Americans were a decisive factor in the final move against Mubarak, but so, too, was the degree of already existing army disenchantment with the regime and above all with the prospect of Gamal Mubarak's succession. Another factor is less easy to measure: the insistence of the "moderate opposition" forces that had joined the protests—ElBaradei, Ayman Nour, senior Muslim Brotherhood leaders—that the movement would respect the unity of the army command structure and deal only with the top brass and not the more radical junior officers, with whom April 6 activists had been building links in hopes of opening the door to a more thoroughgoing overhaul of the regime. The result has been a political hybrid. Asef Bayat, in a piece called "Refo-lutions," published on the Jadaliyya Web site, has nicely analyzed the outcomes in Tunisia and Egypt: their effective delegitimizing of the old order goes beyond reformism—that is, the strategy of pressuring a regime to change itself—yet, lacking the parties and mass organizations necessary to create dual-power structures, they have not been able to achieve a revolutionary overthrow of it, either. The result is that the vast bulk of the old-regime institutions—security forces, government ministries, ruling party, media—are still intact, and the social forces that overthrew the dictatorships have no direct leverage over them. The advantages of this are that there is no immediate regression to social breakdown, counterrevolutionary violence is, to some extent at least, kept in check, and the movements win time to organize wider social forces and exert pressure on the interim regime. Yet the task of dismantling the dictatorship's institutions remains in the hands of the army, and any advances are vulnerable to reverse.

In many respects, the pace of reform remains glacial. The SMC and the state media have collaborated in a "forgive and forget" campaign; the populace has received text messages asking it to "give the police another chance." Though one layer of ministers has been sacked, and charges brought against Adli and others—so far, only charges of corruption, not of murder or torture—Mubarak himself still basks in luxury in the presidential palace at Sharm el-Sheikh, and Suleiman is still at large. But as in Tunisia, the movement remains mobilized: February 11 brought a euphoric release of popular energy. Students and workers are organizing; residents in the informal zones of Cairo's "mushroom city" are campaigning for the removal of NDP-appointed local officials; small farmers are forming cooperatives; and the wave of wild-cat strikes that erupted in the final days of Mubarak's regime continues, despite persistent calls from the junta to get back to work. The January 25 Coalition and other groups have been organized into the Front for the Tahrir Revolution, and are channeling fresh demands to the SMC. On March 3, Mubarak's prime minister—retained by the army—was ousted under popular pressure. New ministerial appointments were made from a list proposed by the movement: Essam Sharaf as interim prime minister, and as interior minister, Mansour el-Essawi, whose first move was to dissolve the political police, the State Security Investigations Sector. At the end of March, the SMC suddenly announced that Mubarak was under house arrest.

What of the junta's positive program? The logic of its moves to date seems to point to a more acceptable version of Mubarakism, with the Muslim Brotherhood granted a legitimate—and legitimating—role. The SMC integrated MB figures into the panel chosen to draft constitutional amendments, which were put to referendum on March 19. The timetable this envisages looks set to give the Brotherhood substantial weight in the new legislature —first-past-the-post parliamentary elections are penciled in for September 2011—and in the constituent assembly that the panel will then appoint. Real power will still lie with the president, who is likely to be elected by the end of the year, but the victorious candidate will depend on MB votes. The Egyptian Brotherhood has long enjoyed a much cozier relationship with the military than the Turkish Islamists have ever had: its senior leadership collaborated shamelessly with Mubarak whenever it got the chance, even voting in Parliament for his self-succession, and was happy to enter negotiations with Suleiman even as police thugs assaulted demonstrators in Tahrir Square. On the other hand, the Brotherhood's younger layer is more restless and radical. So the movement in Egypt could see a split in the opposite direction from its counterpart in Turkey, where the openly pro-capitalist, "moderate" younger generation around Erdoğan and Gul broke away from the anti-imperialist old guard around Erbakan to form the AKP—the political expression of a rising "Anatolian Tiger" business class, eager to ride the globalization boom, that has no equivalent in Egypt's stagnating economy. Apart from any domestic issues, one fault line within the MB is likely to be policy towards Israel—a red line for the army and the US which its leadership will be disinclined to cross but which younger militants might well challenge.

In Libya, the protests moved so quickly to armed rebellion that social questions had no chance to arise. They are in any case complicated by the presence of a large migrant workforce, comparable to those of the Gulf States, and by local resentments at Gaddafi's personalized and politicized distribution of oil rents. The initial protest on February 15 was a demonstration by Benghazi lawyers against the latest depredations by intelligence chief Abdullah Sanussi. Mass protests spread rapidly to Misurata, Beida, and then Tripoli, and were met by tear gas and live fire. The decisive shift toward civil war came on February 21, as riot police charged protesters in Tripoli's Green Square, while the "moderate son," Saif Gaddafi—doctor of global governance at the London School of Economics, courtesy of a Harvard team (Michael Porter, Daniel Yergin, and Anne-Marie Slaughter) who, among other services, helped forge his dissertation—warned in a rambling TV address that the regime would fight to the last bullet. It was not a boast, but a deadly threat.

There is an Anglo-Saxon myth that desert societies are simple things. Libya, like Iraq, is extremely complex, and a century of troubles has only made it more so. The Ottoman provinces of Tripolitania, Fezzan, and Cyrenaica had put up the fiercest resistance of any in the Maghreb to colonial incursion. After the loss of Algiers in 1830, the Porte had replaced the Tripolitanian dynast with a professional military governor, who built forts throughout the region and engaged the powerful Sanussi Sufi order to defend the eastern province, Cyrenaica. The Italian expeditionary force launched in 1911, with the support of the Entente, soon ran into trouble: the Young Turks—Enver Bey, Mustafa Kemal—arrived in person to drill the volunteers. Libyan forces kept the Italians pinned to the coastal cities until 1918. Mussolini launched a reconquest in 1923; his army burned crops, destroyed wells and flocks, subjected villages to aerial bombardment, and hanged rebels. The damage wreaked was on a genocidal scale: between 1911 and 1943 the Libyan population was halved by disease, starvation, butchery, and displacement: tens of thousands were imprisoned with their animals in desert concentration camps, and thousands more were brigaded into forced labor units to build futurist villages for Mussolini's colons. Ottoman social and administrative structures were obliterated, and the desert was strengthened, compared with the devastated towns; family- and tribe-based linkages were the only networks that remained.

The British occupied the country in 1943, after winning the Desert War, and installed as king a Sanussi leader who had been in exile with them in Cairo. Idris I was accused of favoring his Cyrenaican cronies and doing nothing for the mass of his impoverished subjects in Tripoli. In 1969 the young officers of the Revolutionary Command Council took power in a bloodless coup, allegedly with British approval. Despite some popular support, there was no mass mobilization. Gaddafi soon began exercising the former monarch's power to make major appointments. Oil wealth was used to build up security services and a new tribal elite. The anti-imperialist rhetoric of Gaddafi's *Green Books* substituted for serious social and political reforms; his deliberate refusal to modernize Libya was most starkly shown in his careful maintenance of the country's labyrinthine tribal structure. After the army made successive attempts to replace him, he dispatched it to Chad, where it suffered a devastating defeat in 1986 at the hands of French and US proxies. The military was then sidelined and effectively replaced by Special Brigades under the personal command of Gaddafi's sons. Gaddafi's reintegration into Western circuits followed his murderous repression of jihadists returning from Afghanistan in the mid-1990s, a repression that he soon extended to Salafists and Muslim Brothers, who were arrested and tortured en masse; in 1996, more than a thousand Islamists were slaughtered during a riot at Tripoli's Abu Salim Prison. Impressed by his penetration of trans-African jihadi networks, the CIA established regular contact soon after. By 2003, Gaddafi was a leading ally of the West in the war on terror.

Now, the opposition to Gaddafi is correspondingly heterogeneous: persecuted Islamists, disgruntled Cyrenaicans of all classes, liberals, leftists, regime defectors, and generals from the ill-funded army. The Colonel was reportedly astonished that his new Western friends had turned against him simply for putting them down: "What do they expect? It's an armed rebellion."

Calls for the imposition of a no-fly zone over Libya swiftly united the most belligerent of liberal-imperialist ideologies, military humanitarianism, with the most cynical political motives —Sarkozy's need for a pre-election boost after the Tunisian uprising had shed unaccustomed light on the lucrative links between his government and Ben Ali's—and the most reactionary Arab forces, the flyblown monarchies of the Gulf Cooperation Council, with Qatar's Al-Jazeera enthusiastically banging the drum. The motives of the Saudis and Qataris are personal: Gaddafi's weightless grandstanding has long got on their nerves. (During one Arab summit a Saudi prince snapped at him, "We all know which intelligence agency put you in power.") At the Arab League, Moussa tremulously applied the rubber stamp. Lebanon, now under a Hezbollah-backed government, proposed the UNSC resolution authorizing the assault. Writing in the *Financial Times*, Paddy Ashdown, lately NATO's governor-general of Bosnia, dismissed any talk of bringing democracy to the Libyans—that would only discomfort important Gulf allies, who were crushing their own protest movement in Bahrain even as Operation Dawn Odyssey launched its first missiles. The only strategic rationale for the NATO bombardment—still ongoing at the time of writing—lies in its reassertion of Western control, subordinating an inchoate and unruly revolt to a well-known narrative, while making plain to the Middle East's peoples that any further changes will require US approval.

Since the Libyan opposition seems incapable of taking any government-held town on its own, and the West has left itself little room to negotiate with Gaddafi should he accept the terms of UNSC Resolution 1973, there seem to be only two possible outcomes: stalemate and de facto partition, with Gaddafi hunkering down in a rump Tripolitania and the Benghazi-based Transitional National Council running the less populated east, or else an all-out NATO assault on Tripoli, followed by the installation of a Cyrenaican puppet (probably a Western agent originally inserted in the *ancien* regime, of which there are many), which would be a rerun of the British implantation of King Idris and, for that matter, Gaddafi. The US is well advanced in the creation of an incipient client regime: the newly appointed prime minister of the Benghazi rebels, Mahmoud Jibril (alma mater: University of Pittsburgh), met Clinton on March 15, three days before the bombing started. Either way, this can only end badly, in a defeat for the Libyan people. Liberal academics in Euro-America who peeled away from previous antiwar positions to support NATO's "humanitarian" mission may yet regret their sudden conversion.

In Bahrain, a US naval base, demonstrations that began with a few hundred activists making political demands—"Down with Khalifah ibn Sulman" (Bahrain's eternal prime minister—at a February 14 Day of Rage, rapidly swelled to a 10,000-member protest against police repression, after a boy was shot dead and the Khalifahs' security forces opened fire on his funeral procession the following day. The Pearl Roundabout in Manama was occupied by demonstrators, attacked by thugs, and then retaken. The following weeks saw 100,000 Bahrainis in the streets demanding the downfall of the regime and answering the familiar scaremongering from the palace—that this was the work of Islamists in Tehran, stirring up coreligionists to install a Shiite Republic off the Saudi coast—with the chant: "Neither Shia nor Sunni, we are Bahraini!"

Like the Balkans, the eastern shores of the Arabian Peninsula have historically lain at the intersection of empires whose capitals were far away. The Khalifas were signed up as Protectorate rulers by the British in the 1860s not least because their fragile position as Sunni newcomers, who had seized the archipelago only forty years before, and their hostility to ancient Persian claims of sovereignty made them ideal clients; they would always be dependent on support from an outside power to maintain their sway over the peninsula's largely Shia population of pearl divers and fishermen. On gaining independence from Britain in 1971, Bahrainis demanded the right to settle the question of their sovereignty themselves, by referendum—the Shah had tried to assert Iran's interest over the archipelago—but their claims were squashed by the UN. An opinion poll was permitted, however, that showed Bahrainis' overwhelming support for sovereign independence against rule from Tehran. Yet the Khalifas' disingenuous claims have been used to justify blocking any representational government. As elsewhere in the Gulf, in Bahrain all key ministries are manned by members of the ruler's family: Prince Khalifah ibn Sulman al-Khalifah has been prime minister for forty years. A massive US naval base is currently home to the Fifth Fleet; within easy striking distance of Iran, it has been a hub for American operations in Iraq, Afghanistan and the Indian Ocean. Anger has been brewing for decades at the discrimination practiced by the ruling caste against the million-strong Shia population, discrimination that can be seen in the run-down housing standing in the shadow of the glass financial palaces and massive oil terminals that blight the islands, in the chronic youth unemployment, and in the brutal policing by a force staffed by Pakistanis and Yemenis with no loyalties to the local community—a practice introduced by the British and institutionalized by the Khalifas. In 1997 the UN Human Rights Commission reported on the treatment to which democratic activists were subjected: suspension of the limbs in contorted positions, accompanied by severe beatings; immersion in water to the point of near-drowning; holes gouged in the body by electric drills. Many of the political prisoners briefly released in 2011, thanks to pressure from the mass movement, have been retaken and held since then.

Washington's position, as the protests at Pearl Roundabout escalated, was to restart the negotiations over cosmetic constitutional reform—described by one activist as "stirring mud with a stick"—that had gone on for a decade. Riyadh's solution: Tiananmen. Saudi forces rolled in along the causeway connecting the mainland to the island. Their assault on Pearl Roundabout began on March 16, with helicopter gunships, tear gas, and live ammunition. Tanks shelled the villages and destroyed a hospital where the wounded were being treated. The Pearl Roundabout itself was destroyed. Hundreds of young demonstrators have been swallowed up inside the Interior Ministry's "fort," and several have already died under torture.

The House of Saud has witnessed uprisings on every border— Egypt, Yemen, Oman, Bahrain—as well as disorder in Iraq and protests in Jordan. And Saudi society is not monolithic: each city has its own character; Jeddah and Medina have skeptical intelligentsias and elements of a samizdat literary culture. Its benighted social conditions are well known: women are legal dependents, not allowed to leave the house without a male guardian's permission and banned from driving altogether. Stark poverty persists in some quarters, alongside towering shopping malls. Close to Bahrain, the eastern province of Dahram has often been in open rebellion. Youth unemployment is high, made worse by a severe housing shortage. Yet inside the kingdom the Arab Spring seems to have caused barely a tremor, beyond polite requests for the release of political prisoners. The Saud family, with some 7,000 princelings, is vast enough to constitute not just a dynasty but also a powerful ruling bureaucracy, with a corresponding density of clientelist networks. It is reinforced by an immensely wealthy Wahhabi clerical establishment whose cultural conservatism offers an anti-American ideological defense while its political quietism sanctions collusion on the deepest level.

One of the Prophet Muhammad's sterner injunctions left little room for misinterpretation: infidels are to be kept out of the peninsula. The Sauds fought with the British against the Ottoman Empire and later accepted US suzerainty without many qualms. Each twist and turn they considered necessary to hang on to power was justified by senior Wahhabi clerics. Pandering to power made the clerics ultra-dogmatic on other questions: their denial of equal rights for women, for example, or their refusal to "encourage idolatry," effected by restricting the number of visitors to the tombs of the Prophet and his wives in Mecca. Some of the tombs have now been destroyed (one replaced by a public urinal), but there have been no angry campaigns by Islamic extremists.

Religion is the ideological backbone of the regime and it penetrates every sphere, as described by Madhawi al-Rasheed, a Saudi historian in exile:

> Nothing exemplifies the enchantment of Saudi society like a local television program called *Fatwa on Air*, a special performance normally hosting a religious scholar who responds to questions posed by the public. A woman wants to know whether a menstrual period that lasts for three weeks qualifies as normal menstruation, preventing her from performing prayers. A man asks whether it is permissible to borrow money to allow his mother to perform the pilgrimage. A third person asks whether high heels are permissible for women and … diamond rings … for men.

The repetitiveness and regular airing of these shows reduce a world religion to a set of trivial rituals.

As Wahhabism is the only permissible discourse, Al-Rasheed goes on to argue, differences of interpretation and state policy are bound to erupt. One outcome was al-Qaida, but there is also fierce opposition to al-Qaida within the Wahhabi movement. In an article entitled "The Raging Wolf and the Buried Snake," Khalid al-Ghannami, a cleric who has since changed his views, writes that there are two trends within the jihadi camp: "One prefers to kill openly while the other remains hidden until it is safe to emerge from its hole." As it has in China, in Saudi Arabia the Internet has become the site for heated debates, where the notion of "unconditional obedience" to the ruler is under daily attack. Some posters are even bold enough to write, "our main aim must be to drive the Wahhabis out of the peninsula." Would Washington ever permit that?

The large-scale US military presence in the kingdom after 1990 put this position under intolerable pressure, which eventually rebounded in 9/11. On September 12, 2001, the day after the attacks on New York and Washington, a Saudi woman resident in London, a member of a wealthy family, rang her sister in Riyadh to discuss the crisis affecting the kingdom. Her niece answered the phone.

"Where's your mother?"

"She's here, dearest aunt, and I'll get her in a minute, but is that all you have to say to me? No congratulations for yesterday?"

The dearest aunt, out of the country for far too long, was taken aback. She should not have been. The fervor that didn't dare show itself in public was strong even at the upper levels of Saudi society. US intelligence agencies engaged in routine surveillance were, to their immense surprise, picking up unguarded cell phone talk in which excited Saudi princelings were heard reveling in bin Laden's latest caper. Like the CIA, the princelings had not thought it possible for him to reach such heights.

Washington had taken its oldest ally in the Arab world for granted. In the weeks that followed 9/11, the Saudi royal family was besieged by a storm of critical comment in the US media and its global subsidiaries. Publishers eager to make a quick dollar hurriedly produced a few bad books with even worse titles— *Hatred's Kingdom, Sleeping with the Devil*—that set out to denounce the Saudis. This mini-industry had little medium-term impact, and normal business was soon resumed. On February 14, 2005, there was even a reenactment of the meeting that had taken place sixty years before on the USS *Quincy*, moored in the Suez Canal, at which Roosevelt and Ibn Saud, the first king of Saudi Arabia, signed the concordat that would guarantee continued single-family rule. The interpreter on this occasion was Colonel William Eddy, a senior US intelligence officer and much else besides. Considered too insecure during the "global war on terror," Suez was rejected as a potential venue for the ceremony: the grandsons of the two principals and Eddy's nephew had to make do with the Ritz in Coconut Grove, Florida. A giant gold-plated Cadillac in the Arizona desert might have been more appropriate.

Looking at the Saudi landscape today, you would think nothing had changed. The princes, unaccustomed to exercising their inventive faculties, continue to distinguish themselves by the size of the commissions they procure from Western corporations. This competition is restricted to fellow royals or nominated bagmen. It is usually friendly and always corrupt. Given that weaponry deals with the West cost billions rather than millions, nobody begrudges the Saudis a token $20 million or so by way of a thank-you. Meanwhile, Western PR firms get the regime's message out. At a European airport five years ago, I saw exactly the same press handout regurgitated by the *Guardian*, *El Pais*, the *International Herald Tribune*, *Le Monde*, and *La Repubblica*: the gist of it was that terrorists were handing in their weapons, renouncing their past and progressing well at reeducation schools.

Obama continues to protect and appease this sump of reaction. Like those who preceded him, he does not even pay lip service to the idea of democracy in the Saudi kingdom. The farthest he will go is to politely suggest that the law banning women from driving might be relaxed a bit. Were the country to erupt, there is little doubt that the US would intervene to preserve the royal family.

Dictatorships overthrown in Egypt and Tunisia; Saudi-backed counterrevolution in Bahrain; armed rebellion in Libya, with another NATO protectorate perhaps in the making; simmering discontent in Syria and Jordan, for the moment repressed and co-opted—behind these contrasted national dramas, still unfolding, can any common themes be discerned as a whole? First, the spearhead objectives of the Arab movements have been over-whelmingly political. With the partial exception of Tunisia, the region's pressing social problems have found only limited articula-tion to date. The strike wave continues unabated in Egypt, but strikers' demands have remained largely sectoral. This could change quite rapidly; for the moment, however, there appears to be a general disjuncture between the social tinderbox that fuelled the mass upheavals and the demands they have expressed. So far, the national question has remained largely latent as well; the movements have produced no mass anti-American or even anti-Israeli demonstrations. "Neither with nor against America," was the formulation of an April 6 Movement activist in Cairo; only a small minority in Egypt has questioned the 1979 treaty or the Supreme Military Council's continuing collusion with Israel in Gaza. Part of the reason for this may lie in the fact that contempo-rary resistance to American imperialism has come to be identified with a few holdout regimes in the region—Syria and Iran—that are just as repressive as the regimes that collude with the US and that offer no alternative political model to them. The NATO operation in Libya is arousing opposition from within the armed forces. But in its opening stages, at least, it seems to have played an effective role in neutralizing any reawakening sense of Arab sovereignty—helped in this by backing from Al-Jazeera, the Arab League, Sunni clerics and even Hezbollah.

Washington, for its part, was clearly caught off guard by the speed of the Tunisian uprising and had to scramble to ensure a front-seat role in Egypt as Mubarak's regime began to rock. So far it has succeeded in securing its core interests there—the 1979 Egypt-Israel Peace Treaty, the Suez Canal—through the Egyptian army's high command. The challenge to the Khalifah throne in Bahrain has been put down and a cosmetic consultative process set in motion. NATO has taken over direction of the Libyan revolt. The situation in Yemen is still in play, but Washington is behind Saleh. Slow to get off the ground, the counterrevolution there appears to be gathering force, and repression in the southern part of the country has been brutal, much more so than in Libya and Bahrain.

In Syria, the military has, till now, remained loyal to the regime, and Bashar al-Assad continues to use his father's methods: torture and death. The mind of a despot is closed. It never whispers advice suggesting that unless a state voluntarily gives the people what they are demanding peacefully, they might one day demand the same thing with guns in hand. Despite the stalemate in Syria and elsewhere, Obama will now have to contend with an altered political environment in the Mediterranean. The main rationale given for supporting the pro-Western dictatorships in Egypt and Tunisia—as also the less congenial ones in Algeria and Syria—has been that representational government could install the Muslim Brotherhood in office. That prospect is now on the horizon for 2012. The outcome will no doubt vary in each case: the Tunisian Nahda has so far played a rather different role from the Egyptian Brothers. These essentially conservative parties would pose no systemic challenge to American interests. But still, the political temperature is set to grow a degree or two cooler towards Israeli expansionism. It remains to be seen whether Tel Aviv will respond with sullen acceptance or fresh provocation.

A common theme of the youth-led uprisings has been the hope that by throwing off the corrupt dictatorships, their countries might escape from a historical cul-de-sac and rejoin a common march to modernity—which is loosely identified, if only for lack of alternatives, with the West. But the trend from which the region departed after 1990 has itself now come to a halt. The Atlantic heartlands are still stricken after the 2008 financial melt-down and struggling to keep ahead of debt and deficit crises. The conditions that underpinned the global expansion of the 1990s no longer exist. Within this uncertain international context, a democratic Arab world will need to find its own way forward. Even without further breakthroughs, the weight of Egypt— potentially comparable in its exemplary effect to France in 1848 —suggests that the regional status quo ante is unlikely to be restored. It is to be hoped that the Egyptians and Tunisians will succeed not only in uprooting, root and branch, the means by which Mubarak and Ben Ali exercised power, but also in bringing these dictators and their accomplices to trial, to answer for their worst crimes before the people. Following the norm in the European Union, any external treaties that impinge on national sovereignty should be subject to ratification by popular referendum. Maximum pressure should be put on the parties standing for election to commit themselves to a genuinely equitable settlement in Israel/Palestine, respecting the rights of both communities and privileging neither—that is, either a meaningful two-state solution, with equal sovereignty, land and resources, or else a one-state secular democracy. Since the former is now impossible, the latter, however utopian it might appear at the moment, is the only serious and rational possibility. Both solutions are far removed from the priorities of the United States. In 2011 Obama repeated the calls made by every US president, but so great has been US collusion with Israel over the preceding decades that now even the moderate demand that calls on Israel to retreat to the 1967 frontiers, sweetened with a promise of "land swaps" (read: population swaps), is unacceptable to the bigots that govern the Zionist state. Their current chief, Netanyahu, received a standing ovation at a joint session of Congress and Senate, a tribute to the political and financial powers of AIPAC. Obama, too, will not buck this trend. It's reelection year, stupid.

The Arab people want an Arabia without sultans and despots, a possibility regarded with dread by the Sheriff in Washington.

2.

The midterm shellacking of the Democrats surprised nobody. What a strange spectacle Obama offers. Effusively praised for his charisma and his politics in George W. Bush's recent memoirs, but rejected by the electorate. Perhaps the two reactions are linked. The economic and military policies that please Bush are not popular with many Democratic voters. Many who had voted for Obama in 2008 stayed at home in 2010. Abstentions were predictably highest among youth (down from 18 to 11 percent of those who voted, compared with 2008), blacks (down from 13 to 10 percent) and those earning under $30K. But the overall turnout—37.3 percent of the voting-age population, which includes the millions of incarcerated or otherwise disenfranchised US citizens—was not historically low for a midterm election.

With the Republicans retaking the House of Representatives, Obama's has become one of the few governments to date to get a real drubbing from the electorate as a direct result of the general economic crisis. Up till now, political reverberations from the Wall Street meltdown and its aftermath have been relatively limited (though it could be said that the fall of Lehman Brothers in September 2008 boosted Obama's initial victory). The honeymoon is well and truly over. The fact that the Democrats could not even win the Senate seat in Illinois that Obama vacated when he became president was symbolic. During the campaign, Obama made three visits to Chicago, and Michelle Obama added her own stops in Milwaukee and Chicago, where she headlined a fundraiser for the Democratic candidate, Alexi Giannoulias, formerly a loan officer in his family's bank, which went bust after the Wall Street crash. The president and first lady also appeared in a Giannoulias ad. On Election Day itself, Obama gave interviews to two Chicago radio stations with African American audiences in the hopes of boosting black voter turnout for Democrats. It didn't work, and the reasons are obvious. The president undoubtedly remains an effective fundraiser, but what use is money when his ability to get out the vote has clearly diminished?

Obama loyalists are finding it difficult to come to terms with this defeat. They hope he will recover and triumph in 2012 and then, they think, he will introduce a more progressive agenda. They're going to wait for the Barack Obama that is embedded in their imagination to make an appearance. One can only hope that the 2010 verdict may help to lay to rest the myth, still prevalent in Europe, that Obama is a latter-day FDR, battling for New Deal values against domestic and overseas Hooverites. Under Obama, the vast bulk of bailout money has gone to the financial sector; meanwhile, macroeconomic policy is overwhelmingly focused on the international arena, lowering the dollar and "exporting America's problems," but this also depends on screwing down wages and ratcheting up productivity. As Paul Krugman has argued, the 2009 domestic fiscal stimulus was barely enough to offset cutbacks at the state and local levels. Whatever mix of tactics—cohabitation, triangulation, gridlock, impeachment, or a combination of all four—the White House and Congress now deploy, future deficit-reduction measures seem likely to be cut from the same bipartisan cloth as Geithner's policies: hiking up the pensionable age and instituting further means-testing for social benefits. Similarly, the financier George Soros has argued that the stimulus was designed to boost consumption rather than to help states boost employment through new projects, as was done during the New Deal.

In reality, what has happened is not difficult to grasp. Obama's record on the economy speaks for itself. Ironically, the Obama administration, obsessed with avoiding President Clinton's mid-term fate, kept rigidly focused on a finance-led modernization agenda and by doing so produced a bigger backlash and lost more House seats than Clinton did in 1994. The political capital of 2008 was squandered on a health-care bill written by the insurance and pharmaceutical corporations, while unemployment and fore-closures climbed at faster rates than anywhere in the OECD. The shock of losing Massachusetts in January 2010 appeared to galvanize Obama for a moment: he summoned Volcker to "get tough with the banks" and promised Goldman Sachs he was ready for a fight. But the effect lasted barely a fortnight; the financial regulation bill that finally emerged is a mass of loopholes.

In the White House, the midterm defeat probably came as a huge relief. No more alibis for behaving like a Republican were necessary. All the chicaneries of a sophist could now be abandoned. The Chicago machine could proceed to run the country as it did its city; in Washington, there was to be open collaboration with the Republicans. Obama is a great believer in compromise and conciliation, so this "centrist" doctrine—in fact no different from anything he employed when he had a Democratic majority in both House and Senate—fully satisfied him and his media courtiers. And compared with the Tea Party faction—a mélange of contradictions—Obama would hardly be accused of inconsistency. Heaven be praised that he was in the White House, keeping the barbarians outside the gate. And if he decided to wage a new war abroad, at least he did so with the minimum of fuss and not in the boastful Bush style, as Rachel Maddow sweetly informed us on CNBC on March 21, 2011: "To forego the chest-thumping commander-in-chief theater that goes with military intervention of any kind, that in itself is a fascinating and rather blunt demonstration of just how much this presidency is not like that of George W. Bush." Nor was she alone in thinking so. The mood music, as I indicated previously, matters a great deal to courtiers at home and vassals abroad. They appreciate Obama as a moderate-sounding Republican, even though his social policies are well to the right of Richard Nixon's.

And if wars are now so acceptable to liberal Democrats, why should they balk at sticking with most of Bush's tax cuts for the rich? Here, however, there was a slight miscalculation. A few sanctimonious Democrats, as Obama described them, were annoyed by the fact that the rich were always rewarded and the poor regularly punished. Who were these "sanctimonious" retards? A handful of Democrats with a few principles still intact, some senators and representatives who saw a dim future ahead unless a few gestures and cosmetic measures were offered to the less well off. After all, they reasoned, there must be something a bit wrong with a country where some billionaire hedge-fund entrepreneurs pay less tax than their secretaries. As income equality continued to rise, making a mockery of what was once referred to as the American Dream, liberals were afflicted by a self-induced paralysis, arguing that the rise of the Tea Party and right-wing populism left them with no choice but to support Obama right or wrong. Interestingly enough, Obama revealed a more nuanced understanding of the Tea Party than many of his hysterical acolytes. Questioned on the subject by a journalist for *Rolling Stone*, he replied:

> I think the Tea Party is an amalgam, a mixed bag of a lot of different strains in American politics that have been there for a long time. There are some strong and sincere libertarians who are in the Tea Party who generally don't believe in government intervention in the market or socially. There are some social conservatives in the Tea Party who are rejecting me the same way they rejected Bill Clinton, the same way they would reject any Democratic president as being too liberal or too progressive. There are strains in the Tea Party that are troubled by what they saw as a series of instances in which the middle-class and working-class people have been abused or hurt by special interests and Washington, but their anger is misdirected.
>
> And then there are probably some aspects of the Tea Party that are a little darker, that have to do with anti-immigrant sentiment or are troubled by what I represent as the president.

> So I think it's hard to characterize the Tea Party as a whole, and
> I think it's still defining itself.

No longer. Apart from the libertarian faction led by Ron and Rand Paul, it would appear that the Tea Party is depleted. Many of those who joined it to protest the bailouts to the bankers and the corruption of politics by big money dropped out when they saw they were getting nowhere. Some candidates elected in its name have proved to be so stupid and so incompetent that the rump is now controlled by party apparatchiks determined to prevent Sarah Palin from winning the nomination. Bush Republicans lead the way, backing Obama where it matters and mocking him for not being even tougher on the poor and those who still believe that wage bargaining and trade unions' rights matter more than capitalism.

In Madison, Wisconsin, the Republicans raised the stakes. They had won the gubernatorial contest in December 2010 when only 28 percent of the electorate had voted and many Democrats had stayed at home to punish Obama for the high unemployment. Scott Walker, the new Republican governor, claimed to be in daily communion with the deity, but what he meant by "deity" was the Heritage Foundation and other loony-right think tanks. For some time now these think tanks have been arguing that the public sector unions constitute a threat to freedom—deindustrialization and neoliberalism have already deunionized the private sector, with just under eight percent of the work force joining a union. Walker went on the offensive, proposing a bill that would effectively terminate collective bargaining and neuter the public sector unions. The result was an unexpected eruption of class struggle that saw 100,000 public sector workers and students, angered by the effrontery and inspired by the Cairo protests, marching together in Madison to try to reverse the flow. They sang, they occupied the state capitol, they laid siege to the senate chamber, they demanded an end to the anti-union laws and they surprised the rest of the country. They lost. Comparisons with Cairo were understandable but off the mark. What the Madison movement revealed was that mass mobilizations were on the agenda again, but without a corresponding politics, which made even the most militant demonstrations largely symbolic. The innocence of a spontaneous movement was violated by the primitive response of deskbound bureaucrats, who assimilated it into their traditional mainstream politics. The end result was determined by the abject surrender of the trade union leaders: unable to pull away from their doglike coital lock with Democrats, they decided to go in deeper. Obama himself had signaled a war on the teachers unions by insisting that states pass anti-union measures to qualify for federal funding. The teachers union responded several weeks later by endorsing Obama for 2012. The details of compromises like this can be studied in all their nakedness in the history of most American trade unions over the past fifty years.

Walker was hardly a lone maverick. Republican caudillos elsewhere were part of the project, and in neighboring Michigan, Governor Rick Snyder followed Walker's lead. Their Democrat counterparts (including Jerry Brown in California and Andrew Cuomo in New York) used the Republican measures to force through cuts of their own, threatening public-sector workers with huge layoffs unless they complied.

The Arab streets had seen the despondent and the downtrodden raising their heads and losing the fear of death; they had stopped believing in the omnipotence of their oppressors. In Wisconsin, too, heads were raised. But the movement there, which could have forced a real government response to the needs of most citizens, was stymied by a failure to grasp that the Democrats were not part of the solution. This is, of course, an old problem. But the social crisis in the US is now so severe and the country's capitalists so arrogant that something new is required, something that even the most liberal Democrats are unable to provide. It is beyond their imagination. Paul Krugman was not wrong when he argued in his *New York Times* column, "What Mr. Walker and his backers are trying to do is to make Wisconsin—and eventually, America—less of a functioning democracy and more of a third-world-style oligarchy...And that's why anyone who believes that we need some counterweight to the political power of big money should be on the demonstrators' side." The real problem is that unbridled capitalism rules both political parties. It exercises power through them. It fears no alternative because none exists.

Americans' illusions are disappearing fast, but the idea of voting for the "lesser evil" remains a dominant strategy of the liberal left in American politics, despite all the broken promises, especially on the issue of civil liberties. Many hoped that under Obama the more shocking measures of the Bush administration would be repealed. The exact opposite is taking place. In May 2011 Obama mounted a classic Rumsfeld-style defense of the ordeal to which Private Bradley Manning, the Iraq War soldier accused of passing classified military documents to Wikileaks editor Julian Assange, has been subjected. The press has reported that the military believes that Manning passed on the documents. Obama publicly referred to Manning as being guilty of a crime although Manning had not been brought to trial nor any evidence been placed before a civilian or military court. The next logical step, given that he's accused of treason, would be to kill him—if not on the Abbottabad model, then by driving him so insane that death would be preferable. Dick Cheney is impressed by the new sheriff's zeal: "I think he's learned that what we did was far more appropriate than he ever gave us credit for while he was a candidate. So I think he's learned from experience. And part of that experience was the Democrats having a terrible showing last election."

And as if all this were not enough, this president who soon after he was elected praised whistle-blowers as "often the best source of information about waste, fraud and abuse in government," is currently prosecuting Thomas Drake, a senior figure at the National Security Agency (and a registered Republican) as "an enemy of the state." Jane Meyer, writing at length about the case in the *New Yorker*, challenged the demonization of Drake and pointed out its broader significance:

> the Obama Administration has pursued leak prosecutions with a surprising relentlessness. Including the Drake case, it has been using the Espionage Act to press criminal charges in five alleged instances of national-security leaks—more such prosecutions than have occurred in all previous Administrations combined. The Drake case is one of two that Obama's Justice Department has carried over from the Bush years.

She went on to cite Gabriel Schoenfeld, a conservative political researcher at the Hudson Institute, "who, in his book *Necessary Secrets* (2010), argues for more stringent protection of classified information, says, 'Ironically, Obama has presided over the most draconian crackdown on leaks in our history—even more so than Nixon.'"[7]

7 Jane Mayer, "The Secret Sharer: Is Thomas Drake an Enemy of the State?" *New Yorker*, May 23, 2011. The NSA, she points out, is "three times the size of the CIA,

What was Drake's "crime"? He was not selling military secrets to an "enemy," but rather revealing the widespread fraud, waste and abuse (including instances of warrantless domestic spying) in the NSA to a journalist on the *Baltimore Sun*. The latter paper subsequently published a useful and revealing series—useful for the country's citizens if for nobody else—based on this information. It was a service to the public, but it was regarded by the political-security establishment as a high crime. And Drake must be punished for it, to deter others from following his example. It is the timeless logic of the security state. The political physiognomy of the post-9/11 American republic remains the same—a national surveillance state—regardless of the change in personnel. It is this that is creating the disillusionment. Thomas Drake, too, had hoped for better things from Obama. So had others who thought that the Patriot Act, easily pushed through by Bush in the wake of 9/11, might be repealed. No such luck. Obama signed to renew it for another four years (presumably via the latest technology) in May 2011, from Paris, where he happened to be on a tour of official visits to the vassal states of Western Europe.

Another case in point is that of Cornel West, a well-known African American professor at Princeton, who was one of Obama's erstwhile admirers. West campaigned enthusiastically for Obama and shared the excitement of his victory, even though not being invited to the inauguration rankled. After two years watching the president from his political observatory, West could take it no longer. In May 2011, he broke publicly with Obama. He no longer knows why Obama wants to govern, but feels that the man

and with a third of the US's entire intelligence budget, the NSA has a five-thousand-acre campus at Fort Meade protected by iris scanners and facial-recognition devices. The electric bill is said to surpass seventy million dollars a year."

he once admired is possessed of a lust for power, like a fury that permanently torments him: he wanted to be president and not just once. The serene, sunny afternoon that many in the country had expected to follow his victory will never come.

Most of the political reasons underlying West's critique are impeccable, but surely he was mistaken in reading too much into Obama's election rhetoric. How could he have imagined that Obama's Wall Street funders were not an important part of the equation? Now the hopes their candidate inspired have been definitively betrayed. It is this that makes Cornel West and many others even angrier, with themselves as well as with the object of their disillusionment. As West says:

> "Can you imagine if Barack Obama had taken office and deliberately educated and taught the American people about the nature of the financial catastrophe and what greed was really taking place? If he had told us what kind of mechanisms of accountability needed to be in place, if he had focused on homeowners rather than investment banks for bailouts and engaged in massive job creation he could have nipped in the bud the right-wing populism of the tea party folk. The tea party folk are right when they say the government is corrupt. It is corrupt. Big business and banks have taken over government and corrupted it in deep ways."

An even more damning indictment of the successive Tweedledum–Tweedledee regimes in Washington came from the pen of the African American legal scholar Michelle Alexander, who excoriated the notion of post-racial color-blindness at a time when the imprisonment of young African Americans had reached a scandalous level. Alexander denounced the complacency of her country, noting that seeing Obama in office "causes us all to marvel at what a long way we have come, but as recent data shows...much of black progress is a myth." Despite affirmative action, "nearly one-fourth of African Americans live below the poverty line, approximately the same as in 1968," and the child poverty rate is higher than it was forty years ago, while black unemployment figures reveal an affinity with African states. The figure that is shocking, however, is today's African American prison population. In 2007, 142 years after the surrender of General Lee at Appomattox, the number of African Americans under correctional control exceeded the number of slaves that existed in 1850, before the Civil War.[8] And so when Obama preaches the virtues of self-responsibility to black communities, arguing that this is the way forward and that "too many fathers are missing—missing from too many lives and too many homes...are AWOL...have abandoned their responsibilities...acting like boys instead of men...," he never asks Why? Where are they? Is their incarceration also their own fault, or might the problem be, perish the thought, systemic? A well-orchestrated drive uses the drug laws as a pretext to lock up hundreds of thousands of black people. And might that fact also have something to do with unemployment, on the rise again because of the rigid economic orthodoxy of the Obama administration?

It is a painful truth of the sort that Cornel West insists has to be spoken aloud and understood before there can be any forward movement:

It is a truth that is against the thick lies of the mainstream. In telling that truth we become so maladjusted to the prevailing injustice that the Democratic Party, more and more, is not just

8   Michelle Alexander, *The New Jim Crow: Mass Incarceration in the Age of Color-blindness*, New York, 2010.

milquetoast and spineless, as it was before, but thoroughly complicitous with some of the worst things in the American empire. I don't think in good conscience I could tell anybody to vote for Obama ... we've got to think seriously of third-party candidates, third formations, third parties.[9]

What West says is indisputable, but is a third party possible in the United States at the moment? George W. Bush retired after two terms, immune to the boos and shouts of his opponents. Many Democratic voters felt the need for peace. They hoped that in their new leader they had found someone who could break the country of its addiction to war and big money. The ultra-right-wing media outlets, too, believed (or hoped) that this might be the case, and a sinister gleam emanated from Fox TV and its radio equivalents.

Obama proved them all wrong. Like a schoolteacher with a rod in his hand, he treated his own supporters like children. He knew them well. He knew their weak spots and, above all, he knew they had nowhere else to go. This state of affairs has existed in the United States for far too long. Given the failure of the Republican Party to produce a credible candidate, it is more than likely that a post-Abbotabad Obama will be a shoo-in for 2012. A precarious economy and the unpredictability of history remain his only serious challengers.

And what of the imperial republic itself? Violent, aggressive, insecure, with an increasingly debased political culture, how long can it continue in this fashion? As long as enough of its citizens young and old, their souls overburdened with flatulence, remain indifferent or even celebrate the crimes committed in their name.

9 Chris Hedges, "The Obama Deception: Why Cornel West Went Ballistic," *Truthdig*, May 16, 2011, at www.truthdig.com.

All this could change abruptly. There is no reason to imagine that American history is more static than Arab history was once considered to be. Surprises, a few of them possibly unpleasant, lie in store. The republic needs to be jolted out of its complacency, but by its own citizens.

What might bring this about? Certainly not US foreign policy, since the killing of Muslims is now seen by many citizens as necessary to protect the United States. The mass deaths in Iraq, Afghanistan and Pakistan, let alone the use of jungle law to justify individual killings, leave many Americans unmoved. Liberals prefer a Democrat to do the business. Beyond that, it's all fine. But all is not well on the home front. The bipartisan economic consensus that defends the current financial system might well provoke a rebellion of one sort or another.

The disparities in wealth between the have-mores, the haves, the have-littles and the have-nots have soared over the past three decades. The corporate media creates the impression that an overwhelming majority of US citizens are probably opposed to taxation per se and definitely opposed to higher taxation. But as a recent book by two West Coast academics points out, this is not the case as far as taxing the rich is concerned. In 1939, before the Second World War ended the Depression, 35 percent of US citizens believed that "government should redistribute wealth by heavy taxes on the rich." The figures were 45 percent in 1998 and a remarkable 56 percent in 2007. Progressive taxation—that is, taxing the rich—is an option that neither political party can afford to even consider, so great is their dependence on Wall Street. Both parties have defended the privileges of the very rich, encouraged tax loopholes like permitting certain incomes to be treated as capital gains and taxed at a 15 percent rate. The result is that "in

2006, the top twenty-five hedge fund managers earned nearly $600 million on average, with the richest, James Simons, taking in 1.7 billion…there's no doubt that US tax policy has exacerbated American hyper-inequality," an inequality on a par now with Uganda's.[10]

The capitalist financial system dominates the country's politics, weakening further the democratic shell that it still requires but wishes deep down it could dispense with. And if seriously challenged, the capitalists might move the country more in that direction. All the laws and presidential orders currently in place to combat "terrorism" could be modified to include economic terrorists, those who challenge the efficacy of the present economic model and thus pose a serious threat to the democracy of the rich, in which the right to make money tops the "human rights" list. It would require a huge upheaval from below to challenge the direction of the American economic system. It will not happen on its own, something the German poet Brecht understood a long time ago:

> There are the thoughtless who never doubt.
> Their digestion is splendid, their judgment infallible.
> They don't believe in the facts, they believe only in themselves.
> When it comes to the point the facts must go by the board.
> Their patience with themselves
> Is boundless. To arguments
> They listen with the ear of a police spy.

---

10   Jacob S. Hacker and Paul Pierson, *Winner-Take-All Politics*, New York, 2010.

APPENDIX 1

DISPATCHES FROM THE
EMERGENCY ROOM

I spent my early childhood in a trailer park in Texas, so until I became an emergency physician in Oakland, I thought I knew something about barriers to health care access, and maybe even something about poverty. The Emergency Department at the Oakland county hospital has around 75,000 visits a year—say, 200 a day. It has forty-three beds; because of overcrowding, there are "extra" patient beds in the hallways, which have ended up being designated as official patient-care areas: first came Hallway 1, then, a year later, Hallway 2, and now Hallway 3 as well. At night the ED usually has one supervising physician with a couple of house staff (trainee doctors), a student or two, and around ten nurses; there is double supervising coverage from the late morning through to about 2 a.m., the hours of heaviest traffic.

County hospitals are where those with no insurance go. The elderly and disabled who qualify for federal Medicare and Medicaid insurance may also go there, but they often take the insurance elsewhere. Those who have no insurance, no money and nowhere else to go come to the county hospital. Our specialty is the initial management of everything. There are patients who bless me for my time, after they have waited eighteen hours to see me for a five-minute prescription refill, and another who regularly greets me with, "Yo bitch, get me a sandwich." I did have one patient, born at the county hospital, who lied about his private insurance in order to return to what he called "my hospital," but many more who feel they have hit bottom when they cannot afford to get care elsewhere.

Around 47 percent of the patients are African American and 32 percent Hispanic. We call the Mongolian and Eritrean telephone translation lines on a regular basis. We also see the patients who are not entirely disenfranchised, but fall out of the system when they lose their jobs; most Americans have insurance linked to employment, either their own or a family member's. It is not infrequent to see the primary reason for a visit to the hospital listed as "Lost Insurance," "Lost Kaiser" (the main private health maintenance organization in California), "Lost to Follow-Up" and once, just "Lost," but we all knew what it meant. We see patients every week with decompensated chronic diseases who say, "I was doing fine until I lost my job and couldn't get my meds."

Some of the visits are for true emergencies—there are 2,500 major trauma cases a year. These are usually shootings, stabbings, falls, assaults and automobile accidents; many, if not most, involve alcohol and drugs. In 2008 there were 124 homicides in Oakland alone, most of them due to gun violence; many victims have been involved in violence before. The Emergency Department gets a stream of teenage gunshot victims, cursing and yelling as they come in, swinging at medics and police with arms scored with gang tattoos; by the next day we see them emerge as the children they are, cowed by the presence of their mothers beside the recovery beds. We also see the bystanders, the teenagers who get shot while walking home from school, the elderly Chinese man hit by a stray bullet as he stepped outside to get the newspaper, the mother shot stepping in front of her son—who claimed not to know the shooters when interviewed by the police, but was overheard by the nurse the next day rallying his "boys" for a revenge run. This kind of trauma has a way of turning victims into perpetrators. The first "death notification" I did as an intern was to the mother of three boys. The older two had spent three months on the East Coast with relatives to let a "neighborhood situation" cool off. Less than twenty-four hours after their return to Oakland, they were shot while walking down the street together. The two older boys died. The eighteen-year-old had a collapsed lung, but survived. At his last trauma clinic follow-up, he was referred to social work for "clinical evidence of depression," though at the time there was no outpatient social-work clinic available.

Drugs and alcohol increase all kinds of risk and traverse all social classes, but cocaine is its own special force in this community. Smoking crack cocaine is such a common trigger for asthma exacerbation that we have come to call it "crasthma" at sign-out. At first, Emergency Department doctors were startled when small, wiry elderly women coming in for chest pain tested positive for cocaine on the urine screen. It turned out they were social opium smokers from the hills of Southeast Asia, who turned to smoking crack cocaine when their immigrant families moved them to Oakland. It must have seemed somehow similar, though it turned out to be much worse for their hearts. I recently saw a fifty-five-year-old woman who had been found on the floor by her family in the middle of the night. Her CT scan showed a large bleed in her brain. After years of planning she had managed to set things up to move her family back to Mississippi, where she thought her teenage grandsons, who had begun flirting with gang activity, would be safer. She had been up all night cleaning the house and packing to leave the next day, and had used the cocaine that had likely caused the brain bleed to help herself stay awake.

There are the everyday medical emergencies: septic shock, heart attacks, strokes, deadly lung and skin infections, respiratory and cardiac arrests. These, along with the major traumatic injuries, are the cases the ED was designed for. But most of our patients do not have emergent conditions; they are just ill and have nowhere else to go. The county system has a wide complement of outpatient clinics, staffed by some of the best doctors I know. But the last time I checked, their next available primary-care appointment was six months away. Sometimes there are no appointments at all, just a clipboard where we scribble a name and medical record number, to put a patient in line for the six-month wait.

Then there are the patients who did have an outpatient clinic appointment, but no telephone, and so were not informed when their clinic visit was rescheduled. There are those who have to take three buses to get to the clinic and miss the last one; those who would like to see their doctors, but forget to come in when they drink too much; and others, especially the elderly, who won't come to late afternoon appointments because they are afraid to travel home after dark. Some patients just need prescriptions—those whose medications are stolen, those who finish a prescription before a refill is available because they feel bad and double their own dose, or those who just want the cough syrup with codeine that has become a popular drug of abuse. There are those who have lives so complicated—by three jobs, or six children—that a 3 am emergency visit is all they can manage. They come to the county ED because we are always open and refuse care to no one.

Coming onto a shift, we hit the ground running. There is sign-out, a twenty- or thirty-minute verbal handover of all the patients in the Department, with an update on their status and discussion of what still needs to be done. Most of the shift is spent running around seeing patients and discussing their management plans. But we also negotiate with consultants and admitting doctors, intervene to control ambulance traffic, and troubleshoot staffing issues. There is no official break—we grab food when we can. I carry a portable phone that rings off the hook with referrals and questions. Emergency physicians are interrupted—by nurses, students, technicians, pharmacists and other physicians—every three to four minutes on average (this has actually been studied). There are shifts when I cannot find time to make it to the bathroom.

Nurses—they range from fresh-faced graduates in tight pink scrubs to ex-military medics covered with tattoos—are the front line of care at the county hospital. They see patients first and are responsible for screening the dozens that present to triage at any one time and deciding which ones need to be seen immediately and which can wait. They bear the brunt of patients' frustration; they are the ones who undress them and find hidden wounds and weapons, medications and money, needles and crack pipes. There is a maximum nurse-to-patient ratio of 1:4 in the ED, mandated by California law and rigorously protected by the union. While the limits are designed to protect patients, there is an inevitable tension between the need to see patients quickly and the need to see patients safely. With a fixed ratio and a national nursing shortage, nurse staffing can become the rate-limiting step in the process. Because physicians' orders—on medications, for example—cannot be executed without a nurse, patients often wait for hours to be roomed or get pain relief.

A few doctors rail at the patients who come to the Emergency Department for routine care, but most who have chosen to work in the county system pride themselves on being jacks-of-all-trades, holding steady in the middle of the maelstrom, being a part of the safety net. So when patients cannot get primary care, we tell them to follow up in the ED on our next scheduled shift. I have started patients on medication for newly diagnosed diabetes and transitioned them to insulin before they could manage to see a primary-care doctor. I have prescribed first-, second- and third-line medications for blood pressure. I have seen three generations of women, plus an uncle, in one family. There are a cadre of regulars we know by name; we discuss their recent visits and send around e-mails when they die. So we do deliver primary care; some of us enjoy it, and the patients certainly need it. But in the end, we are simply not very good at it. An Emergency Department is a lousy place to manage chronic disease.

The failure of preventive, primary care creates emergencies that should never have happened. The County Hospital is where diseases become the worst version of themselves: what should have been a case of simple diabetes, requiring oral medication and diet change, presents as diabetic ketoacidosis, a life-threatening condition of acid in the blood. We see severe infection that can only be treated with amputation, but was once simple cellulitis requiring antibiotics; numerous strokes, which could have been prevented through blood-pressure control. While the Emergency Department tries to give patients what they need, it cannot offer them a phone number they can call for refills, a clinic to return to or the chance to see the same doctor year after year.

Frequently, the ED fails to take the whole patient into account. Given the volume and acuity of the patients we see, some stable patients just have too many problems to address in the course of a visit. We talk about the "chief complaint" in medicine—the main reason for the visit. It might be abdominal pain, a sprained ankle, lost insurance or chest pain. When patients start on a list of several complaints, we sometimes ask them to identify the main thing that brought them in that day. A colleague recently signed out a patient to me as "a sixty-five-year-old man with vision loss in one eye for two weeks, seen here four days ago for indigestion, now waiting for a CT scan to rule out stroke." I asked why we had not evaluated his vision loss when we had seen him four days ago, and was told that the patient had not mentioned it then. When we asked him why, the patient said he had been told he could only have one problem. He chose the indigestion because it hurt, while the vision loss was painless.

All Emergency Departments are legally required to examine patients and provide initial treatment, regardless of insurance status; but the definition of "initial treatment" is broad. Frequently, we see patients with acute fractures diagnosed at a private hospital. They arrive with temporary splints in place and X-rays in hand, saying, "I didn't have insurance, so they told me to follow up here." When we want to transfer patients to a nearby hospital for cardiac catheterization to treat a severe heart attack, we are asked to fax over the "face sheet," a summary printout of the patient's basic demographic information: name, date of birth, address, phone number and insurance status. While it is technically illegal for hospitals that have room to refuse to accept a patient who needs a "higher level of care," such as the cardiac catheterization that our hospital does not offer, we are frequently told there are no available beds. We are told this much more often for our uninsured patients than for those with

Medicare, or those who have secured disability payments from the government.

Care delivery in America lags far behind our pharmaceutical and diagnostic science. Most applications for new drug approvals are in categories where good drugs are already available; more than new medicine for diabetes, we need good research on how to get the medicines we have to diabetic people. Our health system has generated an enormous cohort of patients who are diagnosed but untreated, or under-treated. These are not medical mysteries, but social ones. The barriers to appropriate health care are myriad, and not all are a function of the system. I have seen a homeless woman, probably schizophrenic, seeking her first care for a breast mass that must have been there for years before it took over half of her chest. And a man brought in by the ambulance he had finally called when his legs became too swollen from heart failure and blood clots to get through his bathroom door. He hadn't been outside in a decade. Or the young man who had been diagnosed with mild renal failure two years earlier and re-presented with a complication so severe that the kidney specialist I called told me he had only seen it once before, thirty years ago in rural India. The young man seemed reasonable—he was responsible enough to hold two jobs and support one family in the US and two in Mexico. He spoke no English and had not really understood that he was supposed to come back. Until he had become too weak to work, he had just carried on. These are patients disenfranchised by much more than the health care system in our country—by a collision of poverty, poor social services and lousy public transportation, substance abuse, language barriers and more.

II

I have recently shifted my practice to the ED of the University of California, San Francisco Medical Center, twelve miles away, for a one-year specialty fellowship. This is a tertiary referral hospital, famous for treating patients with obscure diagnoses, syndromes that only affect five patients in the world; some are named for scientists who work upstairs in the same medical center. The hospital is a transplant center, and many of the patients are on drugs that suppress their immune systems; the very medications that keep them from rejecting their transplanted organs leave them vulnerable to severe, rapidly progressing infections. Many of the patients have heart or lung abnormalities. I recently saw a child with so little circulating oxygen that his lips were blue-black. Before I could put a breathing tube down his throat, his father told me that he always looks like that due to his unrepaired heart defect. They had come for his abdominal pain. While we some-times complained about the simple cases in Oakland, here we complain that there are no simple patients. Chief complaints such as "finger laceration" are inevitably followed by "heart transplant 2 days ago," "rash" by "history of Gorlin's Syndrome," "cough" by "awaiting lung transplant next week."

I have never been cursed at by a patient in the Emergency Department here, rarely asked for a sandwich, and only occasion-ally see a urine test that is positive for cocaine. Patients can almost always get their medicines and frequently have follow-up appoint-ments already scheduled. They can usually list their medications and often describe their entire medical history by memory. I have more than once been told that the chair of a subspecialty depart-ment would be coming down himself because the patient is a

University faculty member or some other VIP—on one surreal shift, two of my first three patients were doctors themselves. I almost never refill prescriptions for more than a two-day supply, because that is the purview of primary care. On an average shift I see at least three patients who are ninety or older, most of whom drive themselves to the hospital. Almost no one seems to live to ninety in the county system.

The health care proposals generated under the Obama administration take as given the profound inequalities in the distribution of medical care in the United States. Both House and Senate plans fall within a range of middle-ground options that legislate for even more money to be paid into the private system in return for only minimal concessions. They neither create the benefits of risk-sharing for the public system (which currently covers the oldest and sickest), nor make the insurance industry take on the total risk pool of young and old, sick and well, which alone would make universal coverage feasible. With insurance mandatory and non-coverage penalized, millions more would be required to pay into the private system, while tens of millions out of the 46 million currently uninsured would remain without coverage in both the House and the Senate plan. The Congressional debate has avoided medical and social realities to focus on rhetorical dilemmas. Reproductive medicine, which should be a matter of scientific standards of care, has been thrown into the package as a negotiating *quid pro quo*.

Health care in America is the civil rights issue of our time. Extended insurance coverage will not tackle the huge social barriers that stand between patients and optimal medical treatment. Adequate primary care would mitigate the devastating effects of these social factors. In the current County system, a patient who misses a bus and therefore an appointment may wait months to get another, and may not even be able to reschedule by phone. In a functional primary-care system, patients who miss appointments—or a patient newly diagnosed with renal failure—would be called back, not lost to follow-up.

It is hard to talk about a middle ground for something that is a fundamental right. Some believe there is no harm in taking what we can get and going from there; but this is probably not true. The insurance industry makes great gains in the current plan that will be hard to reverse. More, the proposals validate much of the profoundly unjust current system, which has grown up ad hoc but which, up till now, has never been explicitly sanctioned as a workable plan by the federal government. To tolerate a disastrous bricolage is one thing, to extol its virtues quite another.

I have been well aware of the fallout our imbalanced system has for county patients; but until recently I don't think I recognized the damage it was doing to the small minority it serves well. On one of my early shifts at the University of California hospital the triage nurse passed me a handwritten note from a patient in the waiting room. It read: "Please help me. My jaw has been broken and I am in a lot of pain. I've been here over an hour and am still bleeding. My hands and feet are numb and I'm starting to shake. I need some care. I have insurance."

The young electrical engineer who wrote the note was in his mid-thirties, used neither drugs nor alcohol, and had never been in a fight in his life. He had been prescribed cough medicine with codeine for a viral illness and had passed out in his bathroom, breaking his jaw and several teeth on the sink as he fell. His injuries were no more and no less devastating than those resulting from violence in Oakland. What was striking was that a highly educated young man could feel that his pain, bleeding and shaking might not get him care in one of the best hospitals in the country, but that his insurance would; could assume that the brief delay before he was seen was due not to the acute stroke and heart-attack patients who had come in just before him, but to the suspicion that he did not have insurance. If even the privileged feel their access to care is so vulnerable, it becomes hard to argue that the system is working for anyone.[1]

Teri Reynolds

[1] First published in the fiftieth anniversary issue of *New Left Review*, January/February 2010.

APPENDIX 2

A NOTE ON YEMEN

I left for Yemen as Obama was insisting that "large chunks" of the country were "not fully under government control," after Senator Joseph Lieberman had cheerfully announced that it was a suitable target for war and occupation. The sad underwear bomber who tried to blow up the Amsterdam flight on Christmas Day had triggered a new interest in the country, and in al-Qaeda in the Arabian Peninsula (AQAP), by claiming that although he was converted to hardcore Islamism in Britain, his crash course in suicide terrorism, mercifully inadequate, had been provided by AQAP somewhere in Yemen.

The British satrapy, eager to please without even being asked, especially if all it involves is bullying a small country with no economic clout, had banned direct flights to the Yemen, forcing travelers to make a detour that added several hours to the journey. During the long wait in Doha I sighted the glossy *Qatar Tribune* [2/13/10], which headlined an impending US–Islamic World Forum. The advance guard had arrived and the front page had a distorted color picture of Martin Indyk, Strobe Talbott and a token Qatari notable which made them all look slightly creepy; a non-story below announced the impending arrival of Hillary

Clinton, Richard Holbrooke, the Turkish PM Recep Tayyip Erdogan and Anwar Ibrahim—Washington's man in Kuala Lumpur —fresh from a sodomy show-trial in his own country. The menu was undisclosed, but I was sure it didn't include Yemen, since Riyadh is the city of choice for forums on that theme. Were Clinton and pals cooking something to force-feed the Palestinians, or a spicy, preemptive, palate-teasing falafel to prepare the region for the main course being prepared to neutralize the "nuclear threat" from Iran? I boarded the Yemen flight none the wiser, but read a few days later that it was the latter and that Clinton had greatly amused regional notables by suggesting that Iran was poised on the precipice and an evil dictatorship was on the agenda to threaten peace and harmony in the Middle East and, she could have added, its thriving democracies in Saudi Arabia, Egypt, Libya, Syria and Iraq. How would the country I was heading for compare to these blessed siblings?

Yemen is a proper country, unlike the imperial petrol stations dotted across other parts of the Arabian Peninsula, where the ruling elites live in hurriedly constructed skyscrapers designed by celebrity architects, flanked by shopping malls displaying every Western brand, and serviced by wage-slaves from South Asia and the Philippines. Sana'a, Yemen's capital, was founded when the Old Testament was still being written, edited and collated. It's true that the new Mövenpick hotel in the heart of the city's diplomatic enclave is reminiscent of Dubai at its worst—when I was there it was pushing its Valentine's Day Dinner menu (First Rose, Amorio Soup, Full Moon of Love Sea followed by Sweetheart)—but in Yemen the elite is careful and doesn't flaunt its wealth.

The old walled city was rescued from extinction–via–modernization by UNESCO (and later the Aga Khan Trust) in the 1980s, and the old wall was rebuilt. The ninth-century Great Mosque is currently being restored by a team of Italian experts working with local archaeologists who are uncovering artifacts and images from a pre-Islamic past. Whether they will manage to locate a small structure said to have been built on the same site during the Prophet Muhammad's lifetime remains to be seen. Sana'a's architecture is stunning, like nothing else in Arabia or anywhere else in the world. Its buildings—skyscrapers eight or nine stories high— were constructed in the tenth century and renovated 600 years later in the same style: lightly baked bricks, decorated with geometric patterns in gypsum and symmetrical stone carvings (wood was unavailable or in short supply). What is missing are the hanging gardens on every floor that gripped the imagination of medieval travelers.

The net result of the West's worries about the AQAP effect is that the US will send $63 million in aid to Yemen this year. A fifth has already been earmarked for weaponry, much of the rest will go to the president and his cronies, and some into the pockets of the military high command. What's left will be fought over by the bosses of different regions. (The sum doesn't include the Pentagon's remittance for counterterrorism, which last year amounted to $67 million.) A Yemeni businessman told me that he'd been taken aback a few years ago when the then prime minister, an apparently respectable and moderate man, demanded a 30 percent rake-off from a deal he'd been negotiating. Seeing the shock on the businessman's face, the PM reassured him: 20 percent of that was for the president.

I wondered how serious the threat from AQAP really was. How many members of the organization were in the country and how many were visitors from the other side of the Saudi border? Abdul Karim al-Eryani, a seventy-five-year-old former prime minister and still an adviser to the president, received me in the large library in the basement of his house. He spoke interestingly and at length about Yemeni history, stressing the continuities between pre-Islamic and Islamic cultures in the region. He complained that the Arabic dialect spoken by the Bedouin of Nejd (an area now part of Saudi Arabia) had been the largest single source for the modern Arabic dictionary, at the expense of the real root of the language, the dialect used by the Sabeans (who lived in what is now Yemen), 5,000 words of which had been excluded by the dictionary-makers. Later he told me that thanks to the Nigerian bomber he had been visited by the *New York Times* columnist Thomas Friedman. Friedman, having asked his questions, went back to the US and told his readers that the city "was not Kabul … yet," but that AQAP was a "virus" that needed urgent attention before the spread of the disease became uncontrollable. He didn't speculate on the cause of the infection. But when I asked Eryani to estimate the size of AQAP, his response was a mischievous smile. "Three or four hundred?" I pressed. "At the maximum," he replied, "the very maximum. The Americans exaggerate greatly. We have other problems, real and more important."

His view was reiterated by Saleh Ali Ba-Surah, the minister for higher education, a grandee educated in East Germany, like many others from what until 1990 was the People's Democratic Republic of Yemen, the southern part of the present state. The two parts of what now constitutes the Republic of Yemen—ruled over for the past twenty years by Ali Abdullah Saleh, who, like Mubarak and Gaddafi, is grooming his son to succeed him—were for most of the last century representatives of strikingly different sociologies.

Whereas armed tribes dominated the northern highlands where Sana'a is situated, workers, intellectuals, trade unionists, nationalists and, later, communists were strong in Aden and its hinterland.

The country had been united centuries earlier under the leadership of the Zaidi Shia imams, whose temporal power was dependent on tribal loyalty and peasant acquiescence. Southern Yemen broke away in 1728; an expanding British Empire then occupied Aden and its coast in 1839 (the same year it began its occupation of Hong Kong). The limping Ottoman Empire snatched a chunk of northern Yemen soon afterward, but had to give it up after World War I. Under the benign gaze of the British, the imams of the Hamid ed-Din family took back control of the north. In 1948 the ruler, Yahya Muhammad, was assassinated by one of his bodyguards, and his son Ahmad, a fierce isolationist, took over. For him the choice was simple: his country could be dependent and rich or poor but free. As he became more and more eccentric—drugged on morphine and spending most of the day with his cronies in a neon-lit room playing with the toys he had been accumulating since he was a child—discontent mounted. There wasn't a single modern school or railway station or factory in the country, and scarcely any doctors.

Bets were placed as to whether the imam's exiled brother would return and bump him off or whether Gamal Abdel Nasser's supporters in the army would lose their patience first. Ahmad was opposed to the Egyptian president's Arab nationalism and in 1960, at Saudi instigation, had the state radio station broadcast a denunciation of Nasser that was bound to elicit a reply from Egypt. Cairo Radio declared war, but before the issue could be decided Ahmad died. Within a week the chief of the bodyguards, al-Sallal, joined nationalist military officers to seize power. The imamate had ended. In Aden thousands demonstrated their support for the new regime, simultaneously making it clear that Britain's continued colonial occupation of South Yemen would be resisted. Fearful of both radical nationalism and its possible communist backers, Washington and London decided that the imams must be restored to power. The British, desperate to teach Nasser a lesson to avenge the humiliation of Suez, were far more gung-ho than the United States. The Americans' main worry was that the Yemeni infection might spread to the rest of the peninsula and that, if the Saudi intervention backfired, nationalist currents might sweep Saudi Arabia itself, severely damaging the monarchy. The Saudis began to nurture the imams' supporters and woo conservative northern tribesmen with a combination of primitive Islamism and cash.

The political and military leaders of the new state in the north were weak and confused. Nasserite intellectuals in the government took advantage of this indecision and finally persuaded the army to appeal directly to Nasser. The Egyptians, with Soviet and Chinese support, dispatched an expeditionary force of 20,000 soldiers. A lengthy civil war fought by Cold War proxies—to put it simply, Saudis v. Egyptians—followed, costing 200,000 Yemeni lives and leaving North Yemen a complete wreck. The Egyptians were men from the Nile valley, and the mountainous terrain was alien to them. Convinced of their invincibility, they failed to take advice, treating their local allies as both inferior and irrelevant; and as the civil war reached a stalemate and opposition to Egyptian methods, which included the use of chemical weapons, increased, working-class dissent in Sana'a and Taiz was brutally crushed. The war ended in an unsatisfactory compromise in 1970. The Egyptians had emulated the Saudis by trying to buy off the tribes, with the result that their power was greatly enhanced in the new dispensation, as was that of sundry divines and preachers. The war had cost the Egyptians a million dollars a day and the lives of 15,000 soldiers, with three times that number wounded. The subsequent demoralization of the army may well have contributed to its defeat in the Six-Day War. In any case, Israel's blitzkrieg in June 1967 sounded the death knell of Arab nationalism.

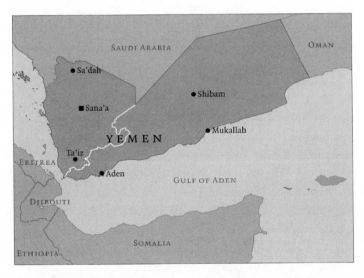

The civil war caused many left-wing nationalists and Communists in North Yemen to flee to Aden. There, British soldiers, French veterans from Algeria, and Belgian mercenaries were recruited by Colonel David Stirling's company, Watchguard International Ltd., for operations behind enemy lines. In the south, too, the nationalists were divided, with Cairo backing the Front for the Liberation of South Yemen (FLOSY) and more radical groups congregating under the banner of the National Liberation Front, or National Front (NF). Both were determined to expel the British, while the British, determined to hang on as long as they could to a strategically important base, increasingly resorted to imprisonment without trial, and torture. In 1964 Harold Wilson had said that British forces would remain in the region but that power would be handed over in 1968 to the so-called Federation of South Arabia, in which he hoped that the Adenese would be kept under control by sultans from the hinterland.

The plan backfired badly after whole villages were bombed into oblivion by the RAF. As Bernard Reilly, a long-serving colonial officer who had spent most of his life in Aden, put it: "Pacification of a country unaccustomed to orderly government could not be effected without collective punishment of collective acts of violence such as brigandage." The leaders of these tribes were unwilling to be pacified. A ferocious struggle now began in the streets of the Crater, one of the oldest areas of Aden. By 1967 the NF was using bazookas and mortars in Aden and targeting military and RAF bases. The Labor government decided to cut its losses and withdraw. "Regretfully," a letter from the Colonial Office informed its native collaborators, "protection can no longer be extended." The Israeli victory in June 1967 did not help the British, since the NF was not an Egyptian pawn, unlike FLOSY, which was gravely weakened. An NF-led general strike paralyzed Aden, and guerrilla attacks compelled the colonial administration to cancel the celebrations scheduled to mark the queen's birthday. Six months later, on November 29, 1967, with the closure of the Suez Canal depriving Aden of much of its value to the British, the British finally left, after 128 years. As Humphrey Trevelyan, the last high commissioner, waved a hurried farewell from the steps of the plane returning him to London, the Royal Marine Band from HMS *Eagle* played "Fings Ain't Wot They Used T'Be."

The National Liberation Front had won, but they had no plan for rebuilding the country. Its members came from different currents of the left: Moscow supporters, Maoists, supporters of Che Guevara, a few Trotskyists and orthodox nationalists. All immediately agreed to establish diplomatic relations with the Soviet Union, and this was done on December 3, 1967. But disputes soon began. The NF Congress passed a motion put forward by the radicals that demanded agrarian reforms, an end to illiteracy, the formation of a people's militia, a purge of the civil and military apparatus, support for the Palestinian resistance and close cooperation with Russia and China. The new elected leadership was dominated by the left. An attempted putsch by the army almost led to civil war, as armed guerrilla detachments surrounded the military camps and disarmed the officers. By May 1968 it was clear that the right wing of the NF had no intention of implementing the conference resolutions. A 14 May Movement was created to mobilize support for the reforms. There were clashes with the military followed by a strange hiatus reminiscent of the July Days of 1917 in Petrograd. The right thought it had won and boasted that "the organizers of the 14 May Movement, having read a lot of Régis Debray, imagined that they were carrying out 'a revolution within the revolution.' " But within a year the left had triumphed.

The 1970 constitution proclaimed the country a socialist republic—the People's Democratic Republic of Yemen—against the advice of both China and the Soviet Union. (In October 1968 the Chinese foreign minister, Chen Yi, himself then under siege by Red Guards, had told a visiting South Yemeni delegation that "your every claim about constructing socialism and raising slogans which are impractical and provocative offer, by their nature, sharp weapons to your adversaries.") What followed was tragically predictable. An economically backward state embarked on creating structures that institutionalized austerity and universalized scarcity. Promoting industrialization via state enterprises might have been helpful had it not been for the imposition of a total ban on petty-commodity production. To this was added a state monopoly on all modes of communication, strict control over what was allowed to be said or published, and the exclusion of all parties other than the Yemeni Socialist Party. It was a mockery both of socialism and of the promises made during the anticolonial struggle. What is undeniable is that the new system of universal education and health care and the advancement of women marked a huge step forward for the region. Saudi Arabia was not pleased.

In due course the neighboring powers—North Yemen, the Gulf States, Saudi Arabia—set to work with Reaganite encouragement on a counterrevolution from within, of the sort then being attempted in Nicaragua with the Contras. They found their instrument in Ali Nasser, a crude, semiliterate apparatchik obsessed with absolute power who became president in 1980. For more than a year President Nasser plotted against the charismatic Abdul Fateh Ismail, his predecessor, who had been a leader of the struggle against the British and who had resigned from the presidency for "health reasons" and taken a long break in Eastern Europe. Ismail still had many supporters among the leadership when he returned from Moscow in 1985 and was soon reelected to the PDRY Politburo, where he commanded a majority.

On January 13, 1986, Ali Nasser's car was seen outside the Central Committee building (a replica of similar monster structures in Eastern Europe), where a meeting of the Politburo had been scheduled. But Ali Nasser didn't appear at the meeting. Instead, his well-built bodyguard, on heavy drugs and carrying a

Scorpion machine gun, entered the room and shot dead the vice-president, Ali Ahmed Antar, before shooting everyone else in the room. Four key Politburo members, including Ismail, were killed, together with eight Central Committee members. Elsewhere, Ali Nasser's men were creating havoc: Ismail's house was destroyed by mortar shells, and there was wild shooting around the city. At 12:30 p.m. Aden radio and TV broadcast that the president had circumvented an attempted coup by the right and that Ismail and his collaborators had been executed. Three hours later the BBC Arabic Service announced that the "moderate and pragmatic" president of Yemen had foiled a coup attempt by hard-line Communists. This was the line adopted by most of the Western media, which wrote of it as the defeat of a Moscow-backed attempt to further radicalize the country, this despite the fact that Gorbachev was now in power. As news of the killings spread in Aden, crowds began to gather and troops recaptured the Ministry of Defense and its operations room from Ali Nasser's men. Battles raged throughout the night. Numerous unarmed Party members, trade unionists and peasant leaders were killed by Nasser's troops: lists had been prepared well in advance. But after five days of heavy fighting, the "pragmatic moderates" were defeated. Ali Nasser fled to North Yemen and later Dubai. He now runs a "cultural center" in Damascus, where he has various business interests.

The shoot-out at the Central Committee meeting was the beginning of the end for the PDRY. The Western proxies in the region who had organized the whole affair now spoke of the socialist gangsters who were running the country. As the Soviet Union was collapsing, negotiations began with North Yemen, and the country was quickly unified, in May 1990, with a five-member presidential council representing both sides. The following year a new constitution lifted all restrictions on freedom of speech, press and association.

The unification did not work out well. The southerners felt their interests had been betrayed, and constant bickering did not augur well for the future of the coalition government created after the election. Socialists from southern Yemen accused gangs backed by Ali Saleh, the former North Yemeni president, now president of the united country, of attacking their supporters in Sana'a and elsewhere. Relations rapidly deteriorated, and there were skirmishes in the south between the remnants of the PDRY army and northern troops. A short-lived but full-scale war erupted in 1994, with the full participation of jihadi groups and Osama bin Laden, who lent his support to Ali Saleh. The southerners were crushed, not just militarily, but their culture and economy too. There were land grabs, urban property was stolen, women were pressured to veil themselves from head to foot ("If we didn't they called us prostitutes and there were many rapes. We were brutalized into this," a woman, whose face was uncovered, told me in Aden).

When I arrived in Aden I realized that AQAP was the least of the country's problems. Most people in South Yemen are desperate to regain independence from the North. ("This is not unification but occupation," I was told on numerous occasions.) The people are leaderless, and there are strong rumors in Sana'a that the old killer Ali Nasser is being readied for a political return by Ali Saleh, who sees him as a "unifying figure." Meanwhile, demonstrations in villages and small towns see the Yemeni flag and Ali Saleh's portraits defaced and the old PDRY standard raised. Repression inevitably follows, further increasing the bitterness. On March 1, 2010, security forces surrounded and destroyed the house of Ali Yafie, who had publicly burned an effigy of the president on the previous day. Yafie and eight members of his family, including his seven-year-old granddaughter, were killed. Government propaganda accused him of having been an AQAP member.

On the night of January 4, 2010, security forces in Aden surrounded the house of Hisham Bashraheel, the publisher-editor of *Al-Ayyam*: this newspaper, founded in 1958, had regularly reported on and published photographs of state atrocities. It had, for example, carried photos of the dead after security forces opened fire on ex-soldiers demanding their pensions. The paper was banned in May 2009, although its offices continued to be a meeting place for journalists, intellectuals and civil rights activists. When the security forces surrounded the building, supporters of the paper gathered there too, and shots were fired in the air to disperse them. Then the building was shelled: the publisher and his family, including two young grandchildren, were inside. Miraculously, they survived by sheltering in a basement room. The next morning Bashraheel and his two sons surrendered in public view, to make it harder for the army to kill any of them. A local activist informed me that "friends in the police" had told him that the security forces had two unidentified corpses waiting in the trunk of an unmarked car. If Bashraheel and his family had been killed, the other bodies would have been planted inside and identified as AQAP members shot during the raid. One guard employed by the family was shot dead as he tried to surrender. His father was arrested at the funeral a few days later. The publisher himself was charged with "forming an armed group." The British ambassador, Tim Torlot, has apparently sent a memo to the Foreign Office suggesting that the irresponsible independent media are the problem. My informant in Sana'a claims to have seen this document. Torlot is notorious in Yemen for having left his wife for a glamorous

American who worked for the *Yemen Observer*, owned by Ali Saleh's press secretary.

When I was there, I traveled through the south, from Aden to Mukallah, and when I saw Shibam I forgot about politics for a moment. This walled city of mud-brick skyscrapers, some of them more than a hundred feet high, is a living museum. No wonder Pasolini filmed much of his *Arabian Nights* here. He did more. On his return to Rome he raved about the architecture till UNESCO declared the city a World Heritage site. Last year, while they were photographing it from a hill overlooking the town, four South Korean tourists were killed by a suicide terrorist from the north. I asked locals about AQAP. One of them came close to me and whispered, "Do you want to know where al-Qaeda are based?" I nodded. "In an office next to the president." In both Sana'a and Aden I encountered similar views. On Christmas Eve the regime dropped bombs and released drones (with US guidance) on two southern villages where, they claimed, Anwar al-Awlaki, the Yemeni-American preacher who trained the underwear bomber, was hiding. They didn't find him, but more than a dozen civilians were killed.

The regime has also faced a rebellion in the northern province of Sa'ada, which borders Saudi Arabia. The highland population there has been harassed by Wahhabi encroachments and, getting no help from the Sana'a government, decided to defend themselves. Tribal militias captured a few Saudi soldiers, with the result that on November 5, 2009, the world caught its first glimpse of the Saudi Air Force in action. (It should be the most powerful air force in the region after the US and Israel, but its planes usually rust away in desert warehouses.) Ali Saleh obligingly describes the revolt as a Shia rebellion backed by Tehran, which had to be put down with force. But few believe this. The Yemeni army had embarked last August on Operation Scorched Earth, which destroyed villages and drove 150,000 villagers from their homes. Because of the news blackout and banning of relief organizations, the scale of government atrocities is unclear. Muhammad al-Maqaleh, a leader of the Yemeni Socialist Party and editor of the party's paper, the *Socialist*, managed to get some eyewitness reports and put them up on the Web last September. He described a military air strike that killed eighty-seven refugees in Sa'ada and accompanied the reports with photographs. He was held without trial for four months, tortured, and threatened with execution. Finally brought to court, he revealed what had been done to him. Sana'a is certainly not Kabul, but if the regime continues to use force on this scale new civil wars seem probable. Were this to happen Obama would undoubtedly support the regime in Sana'a by providing it with more money and drones to kill the southerners. US "interests" might also require a further extension of the "war on terror," and an expeditionary force from Balad base in Iraq might have to be dispatched to stiffen Northern resolve. A more sensible option would be for the Northerners to grant the South a regional autonomy with full economic and political control of their resources without the presence of the Northern military.[1]

1   A slightly shorter version of this article was first published in the *London Review of Books* as "Unhappy Yemen," March 25, 2010.

APPENDIX 3

PER CAPITA TOTAL CURRENT HEALTH CARE EXPENDITURES, US AND SELECTED COUNTRIES, 2007

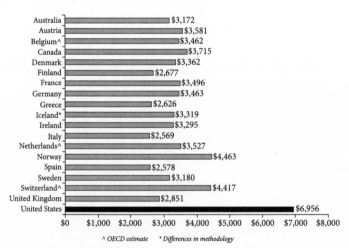

∧ OECD estimate   * Differences in methodology

Notes: Amounts in US $ Purchasing Power Parity, see www.oecd/stst/pop; includes only countries over $2,500.
OECD defines total current expenditures on health as the sum of expenditures on personal health care, preventive
and public health services and health administration and health insurance; it excludes investment.

Source: Organisation for Economic Co-operation and Development, OECD Health Data 2009, from the SourceOECD
Internet subscription database updated November 2009. Copyright OECD 2009, http://www.oecd.com/health/healthdata.
Data accessed on 11/13/2009.

INDEX

201

INDEX

INDEX